FINANCIAL ILLITERACY IN AMERICA: ITS CAUSES, IMPACTS, & SOLUTIONS

By: Eric Weiss

Certified Financial Planner® PROFESSIONAL

ISBN: 1453613390
ISBN-13: 9781453613399

Library of Congress Control Number: 2010908324

Table of Contents

Preface		iii
Introduction		v

Chapters

One	Current State of Personal Finance Knowledge among American Youth	1
Two	Negative Repercussions of Financial Illiteracy	11
Three	Does Teen Financial Illiteracy Carry Over to Adulthood?	17
Four	Implications of Increased Teen Financial Literacy	21
Five	Budgeting: What Do I Need vs. What Do I Want?	25
Six	Using Credit Safely and Intelligently	31
Seven	Understanding Capitalism	43
Eight	Proper Use of Insurance	47
Nine	How to Intelligently Use Financial Services	51
Ten	What a Young Person Needs to Understand about the U.S. Tax System	71
Eleven	Retirement Income – Why Should a Young Person Care?	81
Twelve	How Should a Young Person Select Investments?	87
Thirteen	Different Forms of Business Entities What Type of Company Should I Use in Starting a Business?	103
Fourteen	Economics 101 for Young People	111
Fifteen	Solution to the Problem: Recommendations for Financial Literacy Instruction	121

List of Tables and Charts

1. How Much Retirement Income?   12
2. How Personal Financial Knowledge is Attained   18
3. Fixed Spending Needs   26
4. Time Value of Money Calculation   28
5. Sample Monthly Budget   29
6. Future Value of Money   29
7. Fully Amortized Loan Payment Schedule   32
8. Interest-Only Loan Payment Schedule   33
9. Alternative Loan Rates   33
10. Converting the Annual Percentage Rate to the Effective Annual Rate   34
11. Suppliers of Credit   36
12. Financial Intermediaries   37
13. Demand for Credit   38
14. Split vs. Single Limit Auto Insurance Coverage   48
15. Broker-Dealer Firms and Services   55
16. Money Transfer Identifiers   58
17. Federal Reserve District Banks   59
18. How a Paper Check Clears through the Banking System   60
19. Confused Debt Cycle   69
20. Income Tax Brackets: 2010   72
21. Tax Calculation: 25% Rate Bracket   73
22. Net Take-Home Pay – Taxes Deducted from Gross Salary   73
23. Above-the-Line Tax Deductions   74
24. Below-the-Line Tax Deductions   75
25. After-tax Cost of a Tax-Deductible Expense   76
26. How a Refundable Tax Credit Works   77
27. How a Non-Refundable Tax Credit Works   77
28. Tax Filing Status Categories   78
29. Sources of Retirement Income   82
30. Life Expectancy Probability   82
31. How Compounding Works   85
32. Portfolio Recommendation for a Young Person Aggressive Portfolio   89
33. Examples of Mutual Fund Investment Objectives   93
34. Stock Trading Commissions: Funds vs. Individual Stocks   95

35. Asset Classes and Recommended Investment Products   98
36. Sources of Investment Income   100
37. Preferential Tax Rates on Investment Income   100
38. Types of Business Entities   103
39. How the Fed Changes Interest Rates   115
40. Teen Purchases of Products Manufactured Outside of the U.S.   118

This book is dedicated to the youth of America.

A special thanks to my wife Shelley and son Jason for their patience with a novice author writing his first book.

Preface

This book is divided into two sections. The first, covering chapters one through seven, identifies the negative implications of financial illiteracy on personal finances and the economy as a whole, most notably the financial panic and recession of 2008-2009. The second part, beginning with chapter eight, is a guide for young people to understand and intelligently use financial services in the hope of avoiding a repeat of the calamity of 2008-2009. The last chapter contains my recommendations for introducing personal finance, on a more formal basis, into high school curriculums.

The terms "teen," "young adult," and "young person" are used interchangeably and refer to individuals in the eighteen to twenty-five age group.

By way of background, I am a practicing Certified Financial Planner™ professional, creating personal financial plans and managing investments for my clients. On the side, I teach "Introduction to Finance" to college students at a major university. My experience teaching this course made me think about the need to better prepare high school students in personal finance concepts.

Introduction

This book identifies how young people's misperceptions about personal finance carry forward into adult life and how this has become destructive to the country, specifically as one of the main causes of the Great Recession of 2008-2009.

- Does it matter that most American high school students are functionally illiterate as it pertains to personal finance?

- Does it matter that over their lifetime, American kids will end up spending approximately $2.5 million?[1]

- Does it matter that the average college student has $19.7 thousand of debt when he/she graduates?[2]

- Does it matter that one of the principal causes of the Great Recession of 2008-09 was Americans' lack of understanding of basic financial concepts, for example, the consequences of excessive debt?

- Does it matter that the two most recent asset bubbles, tech stocks between 1997 and 2000 and real estate between 2003 and 2007, were in large part caused by a lack of understanding regarding investment decisions?

The list goes on, but I think the message and the premise of this book are clear: Personal financial illiteracy is not only dangerous to your personal wealth, but is also destructive to the country. Because most Americans are not taught these concepts in their formative years, they find it unnecessary, inconvenient, embarrassing, or unpleasant to learn these concepts as an adult.

If you are not taught a concept, what is the likelihood you will learn it on your own? For example, if you were never taught chemistry, what are the chances you will learn the Periodic Chart of the Elements on your own—something you might browse through on a Sunday afternoon?

Some may say that teaching young people personal finance is too complicated; I disagree. Have you ever seen a teen use his/her iPhone or Blackberry, or figure out how to record using your DVR?

The point is, kids learn these things because they have to in order to be accepted by their peers; it's deemed "cool" or "hip" to use them, so they learn. If as a society we made learning personal finance "cool" or "hip" it too would be a sought after subject.

Others say it's pointless to teach personal finance to high school students because they will learn what they need to know in college, or better, be taught at home. The problem is that according to the U.S. Census Bureau, only 30 percent of the U.S. population aged twenty-five to twenty-nine has completed college. Furthermore, only a small fraction of those attending college will ever take a finance course.

Personal finance might also be taught at home, however, there are two powerful forces working against this:

1. Most parents do not have the knowledge to instruct their children in personal finance. Yes a "penny saved is a penny earned" is good advice, but being able to explain annual percentage rates, present value and loan amortization concepts goes beyond colloquial sayings.

2. Many parents think it inappropriate to talk about money at home and, therefore, do not.

Another argument is that young people will learn personal finance through actual experience. Can people learn the skills for financial well-being on their own simply by doing? Could you learn calculus on your own? What about algebra or chemistry?

The problem is too many people view finance as something they can pick up in life by talking to colleagues, friends, and family. That might be true if everyone was knowledgeable about financial topics; in fact, most people are not. A survey conducted by the Networks Financial Institute, at Indiana State University, found that just 28 percent of U.S. adults viewed their personal financial knowledge as "very good" or "excellent."[3] Another survey conducted in 2003 by the National Association of Security Dealers (now called the Financial Industry Regulatory Authority or "FINRA") on Investor Literacy found a large majority, 79 percent, knew the definition of a stock, but just 51 percent could define a "junk" bond, and only 21 percent correctly defined a "no-load" mutual fund. In addition, almost 50 percent believed that their stock market losses were insured.[4]

One only needs to look at the mortgage situation to realize the serious negative consequences of entering into financial transactions not fully understood to realize this is not a recipe for success. Another example is people purchasing tech stocks at precisely the moment they are most expensive. I use an analogy with my clients to illustrate the folly of this by asking how many would purchase a new suit if it were just marked up by 40 percent. The reason people purchase stocks when they are marked up 40 percent is due to a psychological phenomenon whereby people extrapolate past events, that is, high returns into the future.

Why is Personal Finance Not Taught in Many High Schools?

Though such courses are offered in private schools, most public high schools do not offer personal finance courses. What is the reason for this? I think three words provide an answer: Budgets, Priorities, and Competence.

- Budgets – They are limited.

- Priorities – Other subjects are given preference.

- Competence – Most public high school teachers are not equipped to teach personal finance, and most people knowledgeable in personal finance would rather not teach in a high school, let alone a public high school.

Not teaching personal finance is somewhat shocking; junior and high school students are required to take three or four years of a foreign language, yet not required to understand how to balance a checkbook, manage credit card debt, or use a budget.

Do you need to speak a foreign language for your job? Do you need to speak a foreign language to perform your daily activities? No, yet learning a foreign language is required in high schools. How many of your friends and acquaintances need the knowledge of a foreign language in their job or their daily life activities?

I think it's great to speak another language, but I dare say knowing how an adjustable rate mortgage operates or what the London Inter Bank Offering Rate (LIBOR is the reference interest rate on many adjustable rate mortgages) is would be more valuable than knowing how to say, "How are you doing today," in Spanish, French, German, or Italian.

A summary of what young people (and adults) need to know about personal finance is offered in this book.

Chapter One

CURRENT STATE OF PERSONAL FINANCE KNOWLEDGE AMONG AMERICAN YOUTH

In May 2008, forty-six thousand American high school students (there are seventeen million U.S. high school students) took the National Financial Literacy Challenge (administered by the Treasury Department). Not surprisingly, the average score was 56 percent.

In a 2007 study among American teens, Charles Schwab & Co., Inc. found:[5]

1. Fifty-one percent knew how to write a check.
2. Thirty-four percent could balance a checkbook.
3. Twenty-six percent knew how credit card fees work.
4. Twenty-four percent knew whether a check-cashing service was a good or bad thing to use.

In 2008, the Jump$tart Coalition, a coalition of organizations dedicated to improving financial literacy among school children, conducted its annual survey of high school senior financial literacy by administering a forty-nine question test to over six thousand students. The 2007 average score was 48.3 percent, the lowest recorded since the survey began in 1997.[6]

A review of some questions provides insight into how a lack of personal financial knowledge is damaging to both the individual and the country as a whole.

A sample question from the test was:

Which of the following is true about sales taxes?

a) The national sales tax percentage is 6%.
b) The federal government will deduct it from your paycheck.
c) You don't have to pay it if your income is very low.
d) It makes things more expensive for the things you buy.

Only 42 percent of high school seniors answered this correctly by choosing d.

This is important because, as noted before, a lack of financial literacy not only damages the individual personally, but also the country as a whole. A value-added, a type of sales tax, is now being discussed as a source of revenue for the federal government. If people don't understand how a sales or value added tax works, they cannot be expected to weigh in on a policy's pros and cons.

Another question, asked about pensions was the following:

Retirement income paid by a company is called:

a) 401 (k)
b) Pension
c) Rents and profits
d) Social Security

Overall, 36 percent of high school seniors answered the question correctly by selecting b.

Ignorance on the part of American workers regarding sources of retirement income is one of the main causes many Americans are ill prepared for their retirement. If you don't know what a pension is or does, then it is unlikely you will take corrective action, that is, save more if you are in a job that offers no pension.

One question dealing with insurance asked:

> If you have caused an accident, which type of automobile insurance
> would cover damage to your own car?
>
> a) Comprehensive
> b) Term
> c) Liability
> d) Collision

Overall, 37 percent of high school seniors answered correctly by
selecting d.

This lack of knowledge causes large mistakes in purchasing insurance and
opens consumers to unscrupulous sales practices on the part of some who
sell insurance. It may also result in inadequate collision coverage resulting
in an unacceptable financial burden.

The following question was especially relevant in light of the health care
debate now going on:

> Many young people receive heath care benefits through their
> parents. Which of the following statements is true regarding health
> insurance coverage?
>
> a) You are covered by your parent's health insurance until you
>   marry, regardless of your age.
> b) If your parents become unemployed, your health insurance
>   may stop, regardless of your age.
> c) Young people don't need health insurance because they are
>   so healthy.
> d) You continue to be covered by your parents' health insurance
>   as long as you live at home, regardless of your age.

Only 40 percent of seniors provided the correct answer b.

If you don't understand the basics of health insurance coverage, how can
you be expected to understand various proposals being put forward, let

alone engage in intelligent debate? This may also explain why so many young people do not carry health insurance.

On a question pertaining to investments:

> Sara and Joshua just had a baby. They received money as baby gifts, and want to put it away for the baby's education. Which of the following has the highest growth over periods of time as long as 18 years?
>
> a) A checking account
> b) Stocks
> c) U.S. government savings bond
> d) Savings account

Surprisingly, only 17 percent of high school seniors answered correctly by choosing b.

Once again, financial illiteracy early in life will lead young people to make the wrong investment decisions. Unfortunately, over time this results in diminished wealth, forcing people to adjust downward their retirement lifestyle. Because investing in stocks becomes less risky the longer you do it, failure to begin early on increases the riskiness of stock investing over a lifetime.

The low scores recorded by high school seniors on investment knowledge also contradict what parents believe about their children's money management skills; that is, many parents are overly confident in their children's money management skills. This contradiction is a dangerous one because it results in no action being taken in a situation that is sorely in need of parental action.

If you don't understand the basics about investing, then you also become prey to how the media presents investment topics. Like many financial advisors, I have to respond to clients who become agitated from watching financial programs on television. Not knowing any better, you tend to believe things you hear through the media, causing you to make emotional and, therefore, wrong decisions, like selling stocks as they are getting cheaper and buying stocks as they get more expensive. As an aside, during the height of the financial crisis in the autumn of 2008, one client phoned and said that after watching the television news, how could I assure her that the stock market was not going to zero? My advice was "Please turn off the TV!"

Because teens and young people are very much influenced by visual media, whether on a TV or a computer, they tend to give much credence to things presented to them from those sources. Combining this with their general lack of knowledge can result in disastrous consequences. What many young people (and adults) don't realize is that television investment shows are all about selling advertising, not providing objective investment advice.

Lack of knowledge about investing also makes you:

- susceptible to untrue and inaccurate sales pitches on the part of some in the financial profession; and

- gullible to misinformation passed on from friends, colleagues, family, and acquaintances.

Insight into the current housing crisis is provided by the following question:

Many people put aside money to take care of unexpected expenses. If Juan and Elva put aside money for emergencies, in which of the following forms would it be of LEAST benefit to them if they needed it right away?

a) Invested in down payment on the house
b) Checking account
c) Stocks
d) Savings account

Forty percent of high school seniors gave the right answer as a.

It is not difficult to see how misconceptions regarding the liquidity of a housing investment contributed to people putting money into real estate without a full understanding of the risks involved.

Another question provides insight into young people's understanding of investment risk:

Many savings programs are protected by the Federal government from the risk of loss. Which of the following is not?

a) A U.S. savings bond
b) A certificate of deposit at the bank
c) A bond issued by one of the fifty states
d) A U.S. Treasury bond

The correct answer is c; and just 28 percent of high school seniors answered it correctly.

It is not hard to understand the repercussions of this ignorance on people's proclivity to make risky investments. In reality, because people do not understand investment risk, they are prone to slick sales pitches by some in the investment industry that easily separate them from their money in order to earn a high commission. If you are told an investment is "guaranteed" in some way, even if you do not fully understand the nature of the guaranty, you are increasingly likely to make the investment.

Many people do not understand the impact of taxes on investment returns as indicated by the following question:

If you had a savings account at a bank, which of the following would be correct concerning the interest you earn on the account?

a) Earnings from savings accounts may not be taxed.
b) Income tax may be charged if your income is high enough.
c) Sales tax may be charged on the interest you earn.
d) You cannot earn interest until you pass your 18th birthday.

Overall, just 27 percent of high school seniors provided b as the correct answer.

Not understanding the effects of taxes on investment returns is one of the causes leading people to under invest in the stock market, especially when they are young and have many years of investing ahead of them. If you see an advertisement touting the average return on government bonds to be 5 or 6 percent, not realizing that is before taxes and inflation, you are likely to invest your money, thinking you are doing fairly well. But in fact, only by investing in the stock market will you be able to significantly increase your wealth—after taxes and inflation.

For example, over the period 1926 to 2009, starting with $1 and investing in government bonds, at the end of 2009 you would have $84 on a pre-tax basis while only $16 on an after-tax basis—not an insignificant difference!

This question gives further insight into misconceptions regarding real estate investments:

> Which of the following types of investments would best protect the purchasing power of a family's savings in the event of a sudden increase in inflation?
>
> a) A 10-year bond issued by a corporation
> b) A certificate of deposit issued by a bank
> c) A 25-year corporate bond
> d) A house financed with a fixed rate mortgage

Sadly, only 36 percent of the seniors answered this question correctly by selecting d.

Perhaps this question helps us to understand why so many people took out adjustable rate mortgages even when the adjustable rate was not significantly less than the fixed rate. As most now know, adjustable rate mortgages do not provide protection when inflation accelerates; in fact, they contribute to people losing their homes.

The use and cost of credit is one of the concepts most misunderstood, as indicated by this question:

> Which of the following credit card users is likely to pay the GREATEST dollar amount in finance charges per year if they all charge the same amount per year on their cards?
>
> a) Jessica, who pays at least the minimum each month and more when she has the money
> b) Vera, who generally pays off her card in full, but occasionally will pay the minimum when she is short of cash

c) Megan, who always pays off her credit card bill in full shortly after she receives it
d) Erin, who only pays the minimum amount per month

Only 48 percent of the high school seniors answered d, which is the correct answer.

Incorrect use of credit cards has led the U.S. to have one of the highest levels of consumer indebtedness in the world. Failure to maintain spending in line with income and overreliance on consumer credit has resulted in the U.S. Gross Domestic Product (GDP) being over reliant (about 70% of U.S. GDP is consumer spending) on consumer expenditures, and as we now see, vulnerable to its volatility.

Another question deals with understanding of how credit markets work:

Scott and Eric are both young men. Each has a good credit history and they work at the same company for approximately the same salary. Scott has borrowed $6,000 to take a foreign vacation; Eric has borrowed $6,000 to buy a car. Who is likely to pay the lowest finance charge?

a) Eric will pay less because the car is collateral for the loan.
b) They will both pay the same because the rate is set by law.
c) Scott will pay less because people who travel overseas are better risks.
d) They will both pay the same because they both have almost identical financial backgrounds.

Forty-three percent answered this correctly by selecting a; this was the lowest correct score ever recorded for this question.

This question provides insight into understanding how credit markets operate. People often wonder why credit card rates are so high. In addition to the high losses banks experience with credit cards, the fact they are unsecured (no collateral, for example, land given to guaranty the repayment) loans helps to explain, in part, their elevated rates. Of course, if you do not understand the concept of collateral, and how it relates to the borrowing rate on a loan, you will not be able to correctly ascertain the best way to borrow money.

Another question that provides insight into an understanding of how loan rates are determined was:

> Bill must borrow $12,000 to complete his college education. Which of the following would not be likely to reduce the finance charge rate?
>
> a) If he went to a state rather than a private college
> b) If his parents cosigned the loan
> c) If his parents took out an additional mortgage on their house for the loan
> d) If the loan was insured by the federal government

This question was answered correctly by 32 percent of high school seniors who chose a.

Once again, this provides a fundamental misunderstanding of risk and return within a capitalistic economy. One of the fundamental precepts of capitalism is that your return can only be increased if you take on more risk.

To "connect the dots" one must realize that while we all tend to think of an interest rate as always being a cost, there are those within an economy who view an interest rate as a return—mainly those who supply the money, for example, a bank or other financial lending entities. In addition, you have to realize that anything that reduces the risk of the bank not getting their money back will result, other things being equal, in a lower rate.

In my college "Introduction to Finance" class, I ask the students where banks get the money in order to lend to individuals through a credit card. Many students think the money somehow magically arrives in the bank, which they then lend out. One would be shocked by how many students are surprised when I explain that a bank has to go and "buy" the money before they can lend it.

The following question may help explain why some people are cavalier about not paying their debts, credit card debt in particular:

Which of the following statements is true?

a)   Banks and other lenders share the credit history of borrowers with each other and are likely to know of any loan payment you have missed.

b)   People have so many loans it is very unlikely that one bank will know your history with another bank.

c)   Your bad loan history with one bank will not be considered if you apply for a loan at another bank.

d)   If you missed a payment more than two years ago, it cannot be considered in a loan decision.

Of all high school seniors, only 54 percent were aware that the correct answer was a.

Indeed, if you believe that walking away from a debt you contractually incurred will not affect your ability to get another loan, let alone your credit score, then chances are you will be more inclined not to repay.

Such behavior, while certainly detrimental to an individual, also increases the cost of credit for everyone. As noted above, one of the major contributing factors to high credit card rates are the high losses experienced by credit card issuers. If people believe that defaulting on credit card debt will not prevent them from getting additional loans, they are wrong; this drives up loss rates, which increases borrowing rates and ultimately results in more people defaulting, creating a negative feedback loop.

Chapter Two

The study of high school seniors' financial literacy has identified the following areas of confusion about financial concepts:

1. Not knowing what a pension is
2. Confusion regarding the potential returns on stocks vs. bonds vs. savings accounts
3. Confusion over the meaning of investment liquidity, and in particular the liquidity, or lack thereof, of a real estate investment
4. Lack of understanding of the effects of inflation on a fixed rate investment
5. Lack of awareness regarding how not paying a credit card might negatively affect one's ability to get additional credit

Beyond the negative impact on your personal finances, does this lack of knowledge have implications for the general economy and the 2008-2009 financial crisis in particular?

Lack of Retirement Wealth

In general, Americans do not have sufficient funds saved for their retirement. Research conducted by the Employee Benefit Research Institute shows that among people aged fifty-five to sixty-four, the median value of their IRA/Keogh (IRAs and Keoghs are types of retirement plans, discussed below) in 2009 was $52,220. While the median value was diminished due to the stock market decline, the value in 2007 was only $65,000. Using the same age group, the median value of their 401(k)/defined benefit plans (401(k)s and defined benefit plans are retirement plans, discussed below) was $81,000 in 2009 down from $110,000 in 2007.[7]

Combining the IRA and the 401(k)/defined benefit values gives a picture of the retirement wealth for people within ten years of being retired; this figure was $133,000 at the end of June 2009.

Let's assume a hypothetical person is sixty, has six years left until retiring at full Social Security and that for the next five years, the stock market grows 7 percent per annum. How much monthly income would that person have to spend in retirement?

How Much Retirement Income?

Growth in IRA/401(k) balances $186,500

Projected Monthly Income
Monthly Withdrawals $621*
Social Security $1,500
                                             $2,121

* Monthly withdrawals are equal to 4 percent annually of the account balance, a standard used by many financial planners.

This translates into $25,452 per year, which is not nearly sufficient to live on in most metropolitan areas in the U.S.

Can this lack of retirement savings be attributable to young people not understanding what a pension is? Probably not entirely, as eventually in adult life you become aware of this. The problem is that time and the concept of compounding are two of the most important factors in creating retirement wealth, and by acting early, young people can capitalize on these concepts. When a teen or young person first gets a job, they more than likely do not understand what a pension is, which precludes them from starting to save at precisely the time when it will do them the most good—when they have forty years to compound their dollars! Of course, the financial crisis of 2008 to 2009 has only exacerbated the problem. I remember, at my first job after business school, at a major bank in New York, being mandated to attend a human resource briefing on retirement and other benefits. While I do not recall the exact details, I do remember not fully understanding what was being presented and being anxious to get out of the meeting, thinking it really didn't affect someone in their twenties who was so far away from retirement.

Making Erroneous Investments

If people are confused about the potential returns on financial investments, this will lead them to make erroneous decisions when saving for their retirement. Research conducted by Dalbar, Inc., showed that over the twenty-year period ending in 2004, the average investor in equity mutual funds earned 3.7 percent, while the S&P 500 advanced 11.9 percent.[8] What are the reasons for this underperformance?

1. Investors are affected by "recency bias," whereby they extrapolate the most recent market returns into the future and base their buy/sell decision on this. This results in buying when the market goes up and selling when the market goes down.
2. Misunderstanding the potential returns from stocks is also a factor. If you think you can earn the same in a bond or savings account, then you are more likely to switch out of stocks into these safer investments precisely at the moment when stocks seem most risky, that is, when the market is in a decline but in fact are less risky as their price has declined.
3. Points #1 and #2 above are exacerbated by the media who sensationalize market declines with terms such as the market "cratered" today, stocks are in a "swoon," or the economy is "falling off a cliff," thus intensifying this wealth destroying behavior.

Confusion about the Liquidity of an Investment

One of the easiest ways for you to get into financial trouble is to manage your finances without regard to maintaining liquidity for regular bill paying and a "rainy day" fund. Many young people are confused about the liquidity of real estate. Indeed, media reports of "trading homes to riches" have contributed to this problem. Years back, a home was viewed as a place to live; more recently, in parts of the U.S., homes were viewed as an investment, right along with stocks and bonds. If people then view homes as "liquid" investments, akin to stocks that can be bought and sold effortlessly, then people will ignore one of the biggest risks of real estate, that is, it's difficult to sell it when you want, and is, therefore, an "illiquid" investment.

Surely, people's confusion regarding the illiquidity of a real estate investment is one of the reasons for people piling into real estate during 2003
to 2006. Furthermore, if you believe you could always sell the real estate
when you wanted at your desired price, then then there is little need to
pay attention to the details of adjustable rate mortgages, prepayment penalties, or the meaning of "negative amortization" or when missed payments are added to the loan balance. Yes, mortgage brokers and lenders
were more than willing to supply the loan, but each contract has two
parties: mortgage brokers "selling the loan" and homebuyers "buying
the loan." Since many of the people buying the loan did not comprehend
the risk parameters of their real estate investments, leading them to less
than thorough review of what they were signing, they became accom-
plices to the creation of the mortgage debacle we are now trying to work
through.

As an aside, my wife and I tried to refinance our mortgage in June 2007.
We received an offer from a large regional bank in the Midwest, which
did a lot of mortgage lending in Florida where we live. As many know,
after the closing there is a three-day rescission period, during which the
deal can be canceled. I read the promissory note and did not understand
the repayment schedule; I also asked my wife to read it and she also
did not understand it. For reference, both my wife and I have M.B.A.s
and have each worked in the finance industry for twenty years. It was
at that time that I thought if we can't understand this, I am sure that
most other people cannot either. When I asked the bank representative
to give a clearer explanation, he became irritated and made a comment
regarding my lack of intelligence. We canceled the deal and got another
loan that was far easier to understand. With the onset of the mortgage
problems, I wonder how many people took advantage of the rescission
period to cancel loans they did not understand.

Fixed Income Investments (Bonds) vs. Purchasing Power

What if you invested in bonds paying 4 percent for your retirement,
and your living costs were increasing at 5 or 6 percent per annum? You
would then suffer a diminution of your living standards. What young
people are confused about, and many people don't understand, is that
bonds are also called fixed income investments, meaning your return is
fixed; unfortunately, your living expenses are not. When combined with

confusion about the potential returns of different types of investments, this results in many having to sacrifice some of their dreams in order to stay within a budget. While not necessarily a cause of the financial crisis, this creates a personal crisis for many who have to live within diminished expectations.

Young people, and many adults, have a hard time envisioning the destructive effects of inflation on purchasing power because they have a difficult time understanding future values. As demonstrated below, the future value calculation is not difficult mathematically, but more difficult to understand on a conceptual basis.

From a personal financial perspective, this lack of understanding translates into over reliance on fixed income investments to satisfy retirement needs. If it's hard to visualize that inflation growing at 4 percent per year will eliminate 50 percent of your purchasing power in eighteen years, then you will not realize that putting retirement savings in a CD or a fixed annuity (with no inflation protection) is a bad idea.

In a study conducted regarding financial literacy among U.S. adults, the following question was asked:

> Let's say you have 200 dollars in a savings account. The account earns 10 percent interest per year. How much would you have in the account at the end of two years?

Only 18 percent of the adults answered the question correctly.[9] Herein is the problem with the lack of understanding of the pernicious effect of inflation on retirement income and purchasing power—the failure to understand compound interest. Adult lack of understanding is directly attributable to a failure of instruction in high school.

In another survey, adults and high school students were asked:

> Which of the following investments have the biggest risk of losing value due to inflation?

Only 28 percent of students and 52 percent of adults answered the question correctly, "keeping money in your mattress."[10]

Credit Cards

Use and abuse of credit cards early on creates misconceptions that are carried over into adult life. These bad credit habits are at the root of high credit card delinquency rates, charge-offs, and, ultimately, high consumer lending rates. It is not a great leap of faith to conclude that misusing a credit card early in life will carry forward into repaying, or not, a mortgage, which is at the root of the current financial crisis.

A 2001 study conducted by the U.S. General Accounting Office reported some 63 percent of college students had at least one credit card.[11] Another study in 2001 found that 70.7 percent of college students had more than one credit card and that 68.2 percent received their first card when they were eighteen or younger. Just over half, 50.6 percent, did not pay their balances in full each month.[12]

With ready access to credit, what is the delinquency rate of students compared to the adult population? In a study conducted in June 2002 by the Georgetown Center for Credit Research on "College Student Credit Card Usage," the following was found. College student accounts delinquent thirty days or more totaled to 12.1 percent, while for the adult population the figure was 8.1 percent.[13] The data does not indicate what percent of the adult population in the sample attended college and used a credit card while there. However, the adage "old habits are difficult to break" may suggest that students who have problems with credit cards may be likely to repeat those problems later in life.

Not only is credit card debt destructive financially, but studies have found that 31 percent of students reported that credit card debt affected their concentration on academic work. An additional 28 percent reported that credit card debt affected their decision to stay in school.[14]

Chapter Three

DOES TEEN FINANCIAL ILLITERACY CARRY OVER TO ADULTHOOD?

Does a teen's lack of understanding about personal finance carry forward into adult life?

Do adults move beyond their teen-based lack of knowledge to acquire a strong personal finance skill set? After all, we can't be expected to know everything important by the time we are twenty-one!

However, what if young people's misperceptions about personal finance carry forward into their adult life; this then would be a serious problem facing the U.S. economy.

The problem is circular; studies indicate that the number one source of personal finance knowledge for children is their parents, which would be fine if parents had a good understanding of the subject. However, as you will shortly see, a sizeable percentage of American adults do not understand basic personal financial topics.

How Personal Finance Knowledge is Attained

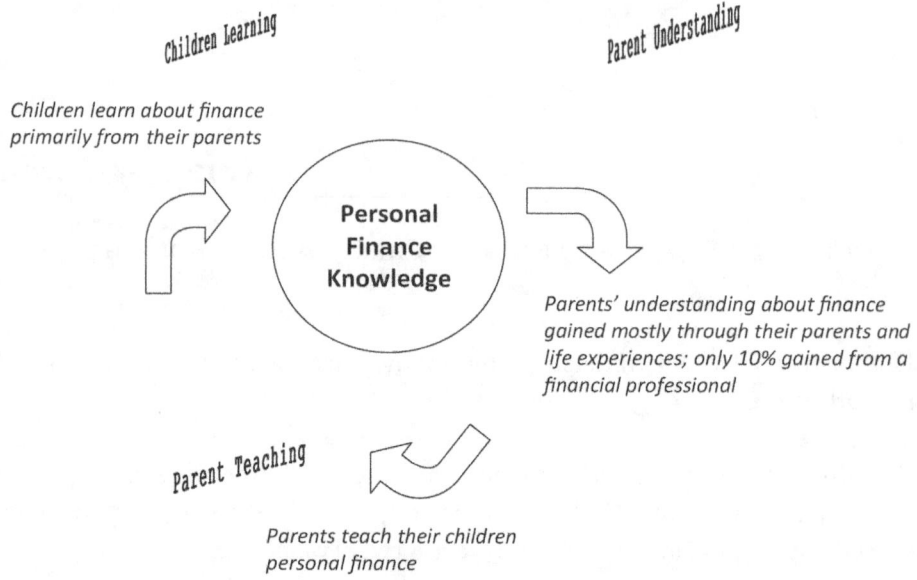

Children Learning

Children learn about finance
primarily from their parents

Parent Understanding

Personal
Finance
Knowledge

Parents' understanding about finance
gained mostly through their parents and
life experiences; only 10% gained from a
financial professional

Parent Teaching

Parents teach their children
personal finance

Parental Understanding of Personal Finance

If parents are the primary source of their children's financial knowledge, how well then do parents or adults understand personal finance?

In a study conducted by Hartford Insurance in 2008, 72 percent of parents acknowledged the responsibility of teaching their children about personal finance, and 44 percent said they needed more guidance about how to do it.[15]

The National Association of Securities Dealers (FINRA today) conducted a survey of 1,086 adults in 2003 to determine their knowledge of investing topics.[16] The following examples illustrate the general lack of understanding of personal finance topics on the part of American adults.

Interest rates and bonds

One question asked about the relationship between interest rates and bond prices, which are inversely related to one another. This is important because many people are under the impression that bonds, unlike stocks, do not change in price; unfortunately, only 40 percent of adults answered the question correctly. This has implications for people's wealth, because experience shows that many people do not hold their bonds until maturity, and when the bond is sold, they may suffer a capital loss because interest rates could have increased from the time the bond was purchased.

Mutual funds

Another question asked people to identify a "no-load" mutual fund; only 21 percent correctly answered the question. Once again, this lack of knowledge erodes one's wealth. In this case, if people are confused over commission and fee structures for mutual funds, then people can be more easily deceived into purchasing a commission-based fund (a "load" fund) which puts more money in the broker's pocket.

Stock market losses

A later question asked whether stock market losses are insured; sadly, only 38 percent of people answered the question correctly. This too can have damaging effects on individual wealth, because if you erroneously believe that stock market losses are insured, similar to bank deposits, then you gain a false sense of security about an equity investment, resulting in taking on too much risk, which can result in large losses.

In another study, adults were asked questions about economics and personal finance.[17] The sample consisted of 3,552 adults of which 28 percent were college graduates, which is slightly less than the percentage of college graduates in the overall population.

One question dealt with the effects of inflation on borrowers and lenders by asking which groups would benefit from inflation. Only 57 percent of the adults correctly identified borrowers with fixed interest loans as the beneficiaries of inflation. In fact, 20 percent of adults thought that banks that made loans at fixed rates of interest would benefit from inflation. It is possible that such confusion about inflation, interest rates, and who benefits/gets hurt creates misperceptions on the part of mortgage borrowers regarding the potential cost of their mortgage. For example, if you take out an adjustable rate mortgage and don't understand the relationship between inflation and rates, you will be surprised, and likely to have not budgeted sufficiently, when inflation accelerates and causes your rate and costs to increase.

In an insight into adult understanding of the effects of inflation on wealth, only 52 percent were correctly able to identify that keeping "cash under a mattress" had the greatest risk of losing value with inflation. Perhaps this, in part, explains why such a high percentage of Americans have so little wealth accumulated by the time they retire. This lack of capital to finance retirement results in people being more dependent upon Social Security and creates pressure on politicians not to reduce or delay benefits. This is a problem because given the current number of workers vs. retirees, payroll taxes are not sufficient to support Social Security's future estimated payouts.

As an explanation as to why non-professional individual investors take on excessive risk in their investment portfolios, a question was asked to identify the attributes of mutual funds. Surprisingly, only 44 percent of adults could correctly identify that mutual funds provide more diversification than individual stocks. Fully, 28 percent said that mutual funds "guarantee a steadier income than stocks." This is revealing, not so much regarding the level of the income, but that so many people hold the view that, somehow, investments in stocks or mutual funds are "guaranteed." As noted elsewhere, this is dangerous because it results in people assuming too much risk under the guise that a guaranty is in place to protect them. Then, when the stock market inevitably declines, people panic and sell at precisely the time they should not—truly a wealth destruction strategy!

There are other surveys showing individuals' lack of preparedness for retirement, not following a budget, excessive credit card debt, and so on. The point is, as the above misconceptions about finance demonstrate, adults do not have the knowledge base to correctly teach their children personal finance. Other studies show a dangerous trend involving a large gap between adults' conceptual knowledge versus the reality of how adult finances are actually managed.

Chapter Four

IMPLICATIONS OF INCREASED TEEN FINANCIAL LITERACY

What constitutes financial literacy?

The level of financial literacy needed will vary according to someone's position. In other words, to be financially literate if you operate a hedge fund with $1 billion under management means something different than being financially literate as a young person in America.

Is attaining a base level of financial literacy consistent with behavior that not only benefits the individual, but also, when viewed collectively, benefits the economy as a whole?

What types of financial behavior would be beneficial to the economy?

1. Budgeting and distinguishing between "needs" vs. "wants"
2. Learning how to use credit safely and intelligently
3. Understanding capitalism's basic principle: the tradeoff between risk and return
4. Correctly insuring assets to protect cash flow and guard against catastrophic loss and associated expenses
5. Being knowledgeable in the use of financial services
6. Being cognizant of the sources of retirement income in order to take advantage of tax-deferred compounding early on—when it will do the most good
7. An awareness of the corrosive effects of inflation on a fixed stream of payments

In the following chapters, we will explore the above topics in greater detail. Here, the question to be asked is if the level of financial literacy for the average person were higher, could some of our recent economic problems been avoided?

Benefits of Financial Literacy

The realization of the fundamental relationship between risk and return as a guiding principle in a capitalistic economy—to get more return you need to take more risk—would be a good starting point. If you combined that realization with a better appreciation of the risks, I postulate far fewer people would have bought tech stocks in 1999, or would have purchased real estate in 2007.

How financial products are sold

Greater knowledge regarding the use of financial services would result in a better understanding of how financial products and services are sold. If more understood the commission structure of insurance annuity products, perhaps fewer people would purchase products that lock them into a low fixed rate of return for twenty years or one with high annual costs and poor investment selection. Better understanding of commission-based sales would perhaps convince some people not to invest in a product that charges them a fee for withdrawing their money before seven or fifteen years.

Fees

A clearer understanding of investment fees might prevent some people from paying money to others for taking and managing their money—for example, actively managed mutual funds—when they could achieve the same or better result without paying such a fee (index mutual funds).

Taxes

Basic knowledge of the tax structure in the U.S. might prevent some people from investing in a tax-deferred product with money that is already exempt from taxes. I have seen people purchase an annuity, which defers taxes on investment gains until withdrawn, within a qualified retirement plan, which also defers taxes on gains until the money is withdrawn. It might also convince them to question the sales claims made by those touting such accounts. This would reduce investment costs (tax deferred investment products, such as annuities, carry high costs) and enhance individual wealth.

Compounding

Knowledge of how compounding works might provide more people with the tools to understand how annual inflation erodes purchasing power and, therefore, convince more not to lock up retirement funds at low fixed rates of interest, thus enhancing retirement wealth and reducing dependence on Social Security payments.

Loan payments

Knowledge of how a loan's amortization affects the total interest costs over the life of a loan might have convinced fewer people to take out "interest-only" or "negative amortization" loans. These loans became popular during 2002-2006 because they permitted people to assume more debt than their income justified. In the case of interest-only loans, no principal was required to be repaid—only interest—until the end of the loan when the principal became due in a one-time "balloon" payment. Negative amortization loans permitted principal and/or interest payments to be omitted and added to the loan balance. Both of these loans result in higher interest payments over the loan's life. Thus, if people had understood the effects of a loan amortization on the loan's cost, then perhaps lower loan delinquencies would have resulted and fewer loan write-offs might have ensued, producing less foreclosures and a healthier banking system.

Interest rates

An ability to calculate the effective annual interest rate might result in fewer people using "pay day" loan or cash advance stores, thus, increasing cash flow to low income people and reducing personal bankruptcies.

Stocks vs. mutual fund risks

A basic understanding of the different risks of individual stocks vs. mutual funds might lead people to reduce the amount of employer stock in a 401(k) plan; for example, think Enron or World Com. Reducing the risk in a 401(k) will enhance returns over time, leading to enhanced retirement wealth.

Life insurance

Understanding the difference between pure life (term insurance) and invest-ment related (whole or universal) life insurance products might lead more people to purchase increased amounts of cheaper pure insurance rather than lesser amounts of more expensive investment related insurance. Also, if people understood that life insurance is a temporary need, this would enable increased amounts of cheaper temporary insurance to be purchased, offering protection for the temporary risks they face. Having adequate amounts of pure life insurance will protect dependents and ensure a family's finances are not eroded in the event of a provider's death.

Fixed vs. variable costs

A clearer understanding of costs—fixed vs. variable—will help people increase the amount of variable costs in their budgets and, therefore, develop workable plans according to their means. The more variable costs—those with the ability to be reduced when income declines—the better protected people will be in the case of unemployment. Examples are cell phone con-tracts and digital movie rental contracts.

Chapter Five

BUDGETING – WHAT DO I NEED VS. WHAT DO I WANT?

Young people need to understand the difference between "needs" and "wants." In middle-class America many people have grown up being given items they want, making it difficult for young people to distinguish between those absolute necessary items—food, clothing, transportation, and so on—and the "like to have" items, such as fashion jeans, the most expensive sneakers, high-end food, jewelry, and the like.

A monthly budget for everyone in the family would likely constrain spending and constrain the use of credit cards. It might also move teens to pursue at least part-time work to enable them to purchase those "gotta have it" wants or learn to do without.

Adhering to a budget increases the propensity to bargain shop in order to get those "wants" let alone "needs." We all know the importance of buying in bulk, purchasing generic, using cash, and so on; conforming to a budget pushes people to use these more frequently.

A budget serves as a planning device forcing young people to develop a short-term, six-month to a year financial forecast. Instilling the need for planning early on is beneficial because it carries forward when the dollar amounts are larger and the stakes are greater as adults. For instance, a keen sense of planning developed in your teens would result in an ability as adults to:

1. Fund an emergency fund
2. Make contributions into tax-deferred retirement accounts
3. Purchase a correct amount of and type of life insurance
4. Distinguish between fixed and variable personal costs

Budgets also serve as a gauge as to when corrective or remedial action is needed. If young people, early on, develop a sense of "righting the ship," then the ability to get back on track due to an unforeseen financial setback will be instilled.

How many times do we incur a financial shock only to become paralyzed to take action? During the recent financial crisis, I have had clients act like a "deer in headlights" because of being knocked off course. Learning an early lesson of pro-active action to get back on budget will later result in more positive behavior as it pertains to one's finances.

How Do You Go About Establishing a Budget?

Know your POP – Personal Operating Profit!

First, list all of the items you spend during a month.

Use this list to examine each item and decide if the amount varies according to the level of activity related to it. That is, which expenses are fixed and which are variable with the amount used? Generally, the fixed costs are categorized as *Needs* and include the following *Fixed Needs*:

> **Fixed Spending Needs:**
>
> - Rent, mortgage, and car payments
> - Insurance premiums for health and on car and house or apartment
> - Cable/Internet and cell bill
> - Electricity, some utilities provide for fixed payments year round, with others it will vary from month to month
> - Property taxes
> - Condo or association fees

In addition, there are certain items identified as *Needs*, but which vary. These include food, gas, and clothes; refer to these items as *Variable Needs*.

The next items on the list are those identified as *Wants*; most, if not all, *Wants* will be variable in nature and include video rental, movies, entertainment, clothing beyond your everyday outfit, music downloads, restaurants, and travel.

Finally, we get to those items denoted as *Wishes*, which ordinarily would not appear on your list very often; they might include overseas vacation, LCD television, expensive jewelry, and so on.

Now that you have everything categorized, group together the *Fixed* and *Variable Needs* and compare this number to your monthly after-tax salary by dividing the *Fixed* + *Variable Needs* by your monthly salary; this ratio should be no greater than 75 percent. If you then subtract the calculated decimal from 1.00 you get another percentage, which is identified as your *"Personal Operating Profit Margin"* or *"POP Percentage,"* which should be 25 percent or greater.

It is from your *Personal Operating Profit (POP)* that you will first pay for your *Wants* and then, hopefully, *Wishes*. Usually *Wants* + *Wishes* are highly desirous items and you will be able to purchase more of them the smaller your *Needs* are; if need be, you can reduce your *Needs* by making some of them variable and then dialing back your activity at times of unemployment.

Of all the items categorized as *Wants*, your *POP* will be spent in descending order of importance until your *POP Percentage* decreases to no less than 8 percent of your monthly after-tax salary.

Your remaining *POP* should be saved in the following fashion:

- An amount equal to 5 percent of your monthly, after-tax salary should be put into an account to be used as a "rainy day" or emergency fund. Deposit the emergency fund into a savings account and invest it in a six-month CD.

- The remainder should be put into an account and invested—to be used to pay for future *Wishes* or *Wants*. Using the time value of money concept will determine the amount of the periodic deposit required for the account. For example, if the account earns 3 percent per annum and you want to buy a car in three years for $20,000 then you would have to deposit $539 per month.

This calculation can be performed with the use of a financial calculator. The functions are: Present Value, PV or what you have now; Future Value, FV or what you want to have in the future; i or I/Y or the rate of return per year; Payment, PMT or the amount of the periodic payment needed to obtain the FV and N the number of years:

> **Time Value of Money Calculation:**
>
> PV = 0
> N = 3
> FV = $20,000
> I/Y = 3%
> Solve for PMT = $539 per month

To summarize, the emergency account is to be used for occasional day-to-day *Needs*, while the *Wishes/Want* account is for longer-term purchases.

What about "big ticket" items such as a car or furniture? You have two options here:

- You could take the amount you are dedicating to *Wishes* and use it to purchase a car or some other large capital purchase, because these items are also *Wishes*.

- Notice in the previous sentence I used the term "capital"; that refers to items that you buy which are expected to last longer than one year. For those items, it is OK to borrow part of the purchase price. The amount you borrow should not be greater than 60 percent of the total price.

When you borrow, you will begin paying interest on the loan. Once you start borrowing, you will add a *Fixed Need* in the form of interest expense. Your free cash is your *POP* and should be at least four times the monthly interest you are paying.

Let's look at a sample budget.

Sample Monthly Budget:

Monthly net (after-tax) salary is $2,900.

Calculation of POP:

Fixed and Variable Needs:	$800	Rent
	$150	Apartment insurance
	$180	Auto insurance
	$50	Health insurance
	$175	Utilities
	$300	Car payment
	$35	Cable
	$60	Cell
	$375	Clothing
	$72	Gas
	$210	Food
	<u>$85</u>	Shoes
	$2,492	

POP = $2,900 - $2,492 = $408; and POP % is 14.1%

The monthly *POP* is $408 of which $145 is dedicated to the emergency fund and $263 is for future *Wants/Wishes*—your *"Wish Account."*

Once again, using the time value of money will show how much future wealth could be accumulated.

Future Value of Money:

If you deposit $263 per month for 5 years and earned 3 percent per year, you would have $17,002 at the end of the five years—not bad!

The budget should be created at the beginning of each year and be used as a roadmap to keep you on your desired financial track. In addition, the budget also serves as a way to monitor your progress and, if needed, take corrective action. Each month you should track your progress vs. your monthly estimated spending. For each month, you will need to establish "trip wires" or threshold points that when crossed will trigger you to take corrective action.

For example, suppose you set up trip wires at a 10 percent level for *Fixed Needs*, which means your monthly spending could increase up to 10 percent more than budgeted without requiring you to take corrective action the following month. Anything above the 10 percent will require you to make it up; that is, cut spending by an equal amount the following month. Anytime you hit a trip wire will result in a monthly contribution to your *Wish Account* being diminished and, therefore, postponing your purchase date for a future *Wish*.

What do I do if I get a raise?

Budgets should be adjusted to reflect any changes in your salary. An increase in your salary should not change your *POP Percentage;* rather, your contributions to your *Wish* account will be increased, bringing your *Wish* purchase date closer to reality.

Of course, large increases in your salary may require producing a new budget as you scale up to a larger apartment or house, more expensive car, and so on. However, the thing to remember is to maintain your *POP Percentage*.

What if I get fired?

This is what the emergency fund is to be used for. With a loss of income, you must immediately refrain from spending on any *Wants* or *Wishes*. In addition, those *Variable Needs* should be scaled back in order to produce a *POP Percentage* (assuming you were still getting a monthly salary) above the minimum threshold. If you are eligible for unemployment benefits, you should not assume this to be a replacement for your previous salary; you should reduce expenses that can be reduced.

Chapter Six

Using Credit Safely and Intelligently

Sixty-two percent of incoming college freshmen have access to a credit card; of those with a credit card, 42 percent reported not paying their balances in full each month.[18,19]

Of college students using a credit card, only 28.9 percent knew the interest rate on the card.[20]

With the abundance of credit offered to them, young people should know how to access and intelligently use credit in our economy. Abusing credit cards and making other mistakes can easily tarnish a credit rating and have a long-term detrimental impact. Not only will a poor credit score curtail one's ability to access credit but could also reduce job and other career opportunities.

What Should a Teen Know about Credit?

1. Loan amortization vs. paying only interest
2. The components of the "periodic payment" in an amortized loan
3. How periodic compounding works and how it affects the rate you pay
4. What is an Annual Percentage Rate?
5. What is an Effective Annual Rate?
6. How collateral, or lack thereof, affects the terms of a loan
7. What causes interest rates to move in a capitalistic economy
8. What an adjustable rate implies
9. When a fixed rate makes sense
10. The main sources of credit in our economy
11. How and what government policies affect the suppliers of credit in our economy

12. How a globalized world affects the ability to get credit and the terms offered for credit in our economy
13. The appropriate uses for credit

Credit is a double-edged sword. Use it wisely and it's valuable; use it foolishly and it can hurt you.

Loan Amortization

Young people need to know, and ideally be able to calculate, a *loan amortization*. To amortize a loan is to periodically pay back the amount borrowed. The original amount borrowed is the *principal*; the amount of the periodic charge for borrowing the principal is the *interest* and is dependent on the loan interest rate and the amount of the principal at the beginning of the period. A fully amortized loan means that over the loan term, or life of the loan, there will be periodic payments containing both principal and interest, usually monthly, to fully pay back the initial principal by the end of the loan. This contrasts with an *interest-only* loan where the periodic payment covers only the interest, and the amount borrowed is not repaid until the end of the term, usually in a one-time "balloon" payment.

How are the periodic payments in a fully amortized loan calculated?

Let's use an example of a $3,000 loan, with an interest rate of 7 percent and a term of three years. The loan agreement calls for the repayment of $1,000 of principal each year.

Fully Amortized Loan Payment Schedule				
Year	Initial Principal	Periodic Payment	Interest Payment	Principal Payment	Ending Principal
1	$3,000	$1,210	$210	$1,000	$2,000
2	$2,000	$1,140	$140	$1,000	$1,000
3	$1,000	$1,070	$70	$1,000	$0
		$3,420	$420	$3,000	

Each year the interest is calculated by multiplying the rate of 7 percent by the principal at the beginning of each period. For any year, the ending principal is calculated by subtracting from the principal at the beginning of that year (Initial Principal) the principal payment during that year.

Now let's use the same loan as above only that the periodic payments reflect interest-only rather than full-amortization.

Interest-Only Loan Payment Schedule				
Year	Initial Principal	Periodic Payment	Interest Payment	Principal Payment	Ending Principal
1	$3,000	$210	$210	$0	$3,000
2	$3,000	$210	$210	$0	$3,000
3	$3,000	$3,210	$210	$3,000	0
		$3,630	$630	$3,000	

By not paying principal during years one and two, the interest-only loan is more expensive because more interest is paid: $630 vs. $420, a 50 percent increase in interest expense!

Interest-only loans are marketed as a way to keep monthly payments down. This is easily deceptive to young people who don't understand how loan amortization works, and the substantially higher cost of interest-only loans!

Periodic Compounding: Annual Percentage Rate and Effective Annual Rate

Young people, and many adults, have a hard time understanding how compounding daily, monthly, quarterly, or semi-annually affects the rate you pay or earn.

Suppose you are considering a loan from a bank; you shop around and come up with the following rates:

Alternative Loan Rates

Bank A: 15 percent, compounded daily
Bank B: 15.5 percent, compounded quarterly
Bank C: 16 percent, compounded annually

Which of these rates is higher?

Bank C is offering 16 percent per year but there is no compounding during the year, thus, the effective rate is 16 percent and is equal to the annual percentage rate or the "APR."

Bank B is actually charging: .155/4 = .03875 or 3.875 percent per quarter, the effective annual rate is $(1+.03875)^4 - 1 = 16.42$ percent, which is greater than the 15.5 percent APR.

Bank A is actually charging daily compounding: .15/365 = .000411 per day or $(1+.000411)^{365} - 1 = 16.18$ percent per year, once again greater than the 15 percent APR.

The *effective annual rate* or *EAR* is the rate you actually pay, and it reflects the effects of the periodic compounding. In contrast, the *annual percentage rate* or *APR* is the rate per period multiplied by the number of periods in a year. For example, if a bank is charging 1.2 percent per month on car loans then the APR is 1.2% x 12 = 14.4%. The APR is referred to as the advertised or "stated" rate; young people need to understand that the APR is not what they are actually paying.

Example: An *APR* of 12 percent on a loan compounded monthly results in an effective annual rate of 12.68 percent.

The conversion of this *APR* to *EAR* is the following:

> **Converting the Annual Percentage Rate to an Effective Annual Rate**
>
> $$EAR = (1 + .12/12)12 - 1 = 12.68\%$$

To summarize, the APR is the rate that appears in advertisements, but it is not the rate you actually pay—that is the effective annual rate.

In order to control their finances and use credit intelligently young people need to know how to convert an annual percentage rate to an effective annual rate. This is the only way to know how much one is actually paying on an outstanding credit card balance.

Collateral

Very few young people understand how collateral, or something which secures the repayment of a loan, affects loan terms.

This lack of understanding leads to young people misusing credit. For example, most young people, and adults for that matter, are unaware that credit cards are unsecured loans made to them. They do not comprehend the fact that the lack of security (collateral) makes the loan more risky (to the bank) resulting in the bank charging a higher borrowing rate. If this were understood, then perhaps many more young people would understand that using credit cards is not a great idea.

Buying a car with an auto loan results in a lower rate when compared to credit cards because the car, as collateral, reduces the risk to the lender.

Understanding the beneficial effects of collateral might lead young people to be more discerning about how they use credit. Perhaps they would only borrow money when the loan can be secured, for example, auto, home, and some types of furniture, which would result in better loan portfolios on the part of lenders, lower delinquencies and losses, and eventually lower borrowing rates.

Supply and Demand for Credit

Interest rates are the price of credit.

Like everything else in a *market economy*, prices or rates are determined by demand and supply. In fact, understanding interest rate movements is no more difficult than understanding how the prices of apples are determined at the local food market.

If you go to your local farmers' market on a Saturday morning and see people crowded around the apple seller, it is likely that the price of apples will increase because demand has exceeded the supply. The supply of apples is limited because the farmer has driven seventy-five miles to get to the market and will not make a return trip. Not everyone who wants an apple will be able to get one; the increase in prices will ration the supply of apples to those willing to pay the higher price. Rationing occurs where the demand for apples is more than the supply. When this happens, the seller increases the price and some people now decide they do not want the apples, bringing about a market equilibrium, as there is now the same number of sellers as buyers.

Understanding where credit comes from, or its supply, will help young people make better credit decisions, notably when deciding between a fixed or adjustable loan rate option.

In our economy, credit is supplied from:

> **Suppliers of Credit:**
>
> - Individual savers
> - Corporate savers
> - Institutional savers or pension funds

"Savers" are people or institutions that have more money coming in than they spend. Individuals get money via their salary; corporations get money via their sales or profits. Individuals spend money on personal items and corporations spend money on salaries for employees, purchases for goods they intend to sell, and advertising for their product.

"Borrowers" are people, or entities, who spend more than the amount of money that comes in. The largest borrower is the U.S. government, which borrows by selling Treasury bills, notes, or bonds. The U.S. government borrows to build roads, bridges, fund the military, and pay the salaries for government workers. Corporations also borrow money by selling bonds; they use the money to build factories, pay salaries, buy inventories, and many other items. Individuals also borrow money by obtaining bank loans, using credit cards, or "borrowing" against themselves by drawing down their savings.

Savings are funneled to people or entities who need to borrow through "intermediaries" in the financial system. Intermediaries are institutions that facilitate the movement of money from savers to borrowers and include entities such as:

> **Financial Intermediaries:**
>
> - Banks/credit unions
> - Mutual funds
> - Insurance companies

Banks and credit unions take in deposits and then lend out the money. Mutual fund companies sell shares to savers and then funnel this money to companies by either buying their bonds or stocks. Insurance companies issue insurance policies in return for premium payments from savers. Insurance companies then "transfer" these funds to borrowers by purchasing their bonds and to a lesser extent their stocks.

People or corporations save by spending less than what comes in. In the case of individuals, wages and salaries represent cash inflows; while for corporations, sales denote the cash inflow. Pension funds do not save per se, rather they receive money from workers and their employers, which they then invest in order to be able to provide income to people when they stop working or retire.

In simplified terms, people will save more when their salaries increase and/ or they reduce their spending. Corporations save more when their sales increase or their costs decrease. To generalize, savings will increase when the economy is growing or when people or corporations are reluctant to spend as they are now. Pension funds generally receive a steady rate of inflows, so they will invest their money at a more consistent rate.

The price of money or credit is not only determined by how much savings there is, but also by the policies of the intermediaries.

Intermediaries, in turn, are influenced by governmental policies—whether the government wants to increase the supply of credit, specifically the monetary policies of the federal government as conducted by the U.S. Federal Reserve. The Federal Reserve or the "Fed" is known as the "banker to the banks" or the "central banker." That is, through its policies, the Fed either encourages or discourages banks to increase the supply of credit. When the Fed encourages banks to increase the supply of credit, then the cost of credit or interest rates will fall; when the Fed encourages banks to decrease the supply of credit, the cost of credit or interest rates rise.

Those policies used by the Fed to either encourage or discourage banks from increasing the supply of credit are known as monetary policies. An "easy" monetary policy is when the Fed encourages banks to increase the supply of credit and a "tight" policy is when they discourage increasing the supply of credit.

If you are deciding whether to take an adjustable or fixed rate loan, knowledge of what the Fed is doing would be helpful in making your decision. Even though the fixed rate loan may initially be higher, if you know that the Fed is discouraging banks from increasing the supply of credit, then interest rates or the price of money will be going up and it would be wise to lock-in the fixed rate in order to avoid higher adjustable rates in the future.

Such knowledge might have reduced some of the adjustable rate loans borrowers took out during 2003 to 2005. At that time, rates were very low and the economy was accelerating out of the recession of 2001 to 2002. In late 2004/early 2005, the Fed began to discourage banks from increasing the supply of credit with a resultant increase in interest rates.

The demand for credit comes from:

Demand for Credit:

1. Individuals buying homes and making other purchases
2. Corporations to buy inventory and build factories
3. Governments—federal, state and local—building roads and schools and paying for police, firemen, and others

The demand for credit is closely linked to growth in the economy: the faster the growth, the greater the demand for credit. Therefore, during a period when the economy is growing, the demand for credit will be increasing. It is during this time that the Fed will likely institute policies to discourage banks and others from increasing the supply of credit. The Fed will do this to prevent the economy from growing too fast, which tends to cause an increase in prices—similar to the example above where apple prices increased. The government attempts to limit rapid price increases (inflation) because people would not be able to buy the things they need like food, clothing, gasoline, cars, and so on. Therefore, it is during such periods that the price of money, or interest rates, will increase.

Teens and young adults, whether they are using credit to purchase a home, car, furniture, or anything else, need to be aware of the direction of interest rates caused by changes in the supply and demand for credit. Making the correct decision regarding an adjustable or fixed rate loan will be very beneficial for one's future finances. If, as a group, individuals are making better decisions regarding their credit usage, the rate of loan delinquencies and loan losses will be lower, resulting in lower consumer borrowing rates for all.

How Globalization Affects the Availability of Credit

We have all heard that we live in a globalized world.

Indeed, actions taken in China, Europe, or elsewhere affect the availability and the price of credit.

Because governments are among the biggest users of credit, particularly the federal government, some of the credit supplied to the U.S. government comes not only from savings in the U.S., but also from savings in China, Europe, and elsewhere. In particular, the Chinese, through their government, are among the biggest buyers of U.S. government bonds, which is a method the U.S. government uses to borrow money; in reality, it's just like the Chinese government making a loan to the U.S. government. The same happens in Europe and the Middle East where governments and other savers in those areas make loans directly to the U.S. government by buying treasury bills, notes, and bonds.

If these foreign governments decide they no longer want to lend money to the U.S. government—at the then current rate, perhaps because they become worried the U.S. government will not repay the loans, the U.S. government will have to offer a higher rate causing interest rates to rise.

When a foreign government lends money to the U.S. government, something else happens, which affects the price of credit or interest rates in the U.S. The U.S. government needs money in dollars, but the Chinese government does not readily have dollars—it has money in Chinese currency or the renminbi (RMB). Therefore, when the Chinese government lends money to the U.S., it must exchange its renminbi for dollars. When the U.S. government repays the Chinese it does so in dollars and the Chinese must then exchange those dollars for renminbi. If during this time the value of the renminbi relative to the U.S. dollar changes, China will have either an additional gain or loss on the transaction. For example, if the initial exchange was 7 RMB for each dollar, and at the end of the period, the exchange was 5 RMB for each dollar, the dollar has depreciated relative to the renminbi. If that happens, the Chinese will incur a foreign exchange loss. Therefore, future changes in the renminbi/dollar exchange rate are one of the factors the Chinese will evaluate to see whether they want to lend money to the U.S. By paying attention to the direction of change in this exchange rate, young people and others can get an indication of the willingness of China to lend money to the U.S. and the future direction of interest rates in the U.S.

Appropriate Uses of Credit

There are two fundamental reasons for individuals to use credit:

1. To make investments in assets with values that will extend beyond the time the loan is repaid
2. As a "bridge" until future funds are received

In the first case, credit would be outstanding for an extended period of time, while in the second case, credit would be repaid as soon as the future funds are received—a self-liquidating loan.

Credit should only be used to help purchase assets whose value will last beyond the time the loan is repaid, for example, cars, homes, furniture, and the like. For example, it would not make sense to take out a seven-year loan to buy a used car if the value of that car at the end of the seven-years is zero or close to it. Loans should only be used to purchase items that will still have a positive value at the time the loan is repaid in full.

Temporary or *bridge financing* might be using a credit card to make a purchase prior to receiving a paycheck or other funds. In that case, anything borrowed would be repaid with the receipt of the funds.

Young people, like everyone else, need to avoid using credit for impulse purchases—purchases you wouldn't make because spending that cash would be in excess of the amount dedicated to *Needs*, *Wants*, or *Wishes* in your budget. Credit card purchases should not be made when you won't be able to pay down or "clean up" the credit card balance with your next paycheck.

In summary, credit should only be used when: (1) it is financing the purchase of an asset whose value will endure beyond the point when the loan is repaid, or (2) as a temporary bridge until the next paycheck or other source of income is received to pay down the loan in total.

Chapter Seven

UNDERSTANDING CAPITALISM

At its most basic, capitalism rewards higher potential returns for assuming greater risks.

There is no way around it; to make more, you have to risk more. This means it is impossible to get something for nothing, for example, "no free lunch."

Young people and others who don't understand this are particularly susceptible to investment scams by unscrupulous financial professionals. The basic problem is people's failure to gauge risk. Once again, because of hindsight biases, past price increases are interpreted as harbingers of the future. Such feelings of optimism result in young people and adults giving credibility to the otherwise dubious pitches of certain financial sales people. The list is long but includes:

1. *Tech stocks in 1999-2000*: When a stock trades at a price-to-earnings multiple of 70, and you are told it is a sure thing with low risk, watch out.
2. *Real estate in 2003-06*: When you buy something under the premise that prices will continually appreciate, after having already appreciated far more than in the past, you should be prepared for a substantial "correction."
3. *Bank CDs*: When told by a bank that your money is safe from the risk of loss due to a financial collapse of the bank, but not from inflation risk, then you must be prepared to lose purchasing power due to inflation.
4. *Real estate as a tangible investment*: When real estate is purchased, thinking it is safe because it is something "I can see and touch," you have not realized the illiquidity risk and miscalculated the risk-reward framework.

5. *Stocks*: Teens often receive money from parents and others as a result of graduation gifts, bar mitzvah or confirmation presents, or birthdays. Often, this money ends up in a stock brokerage account set up as a Uniform Transfers to Minor Act account (UTMA) or Uniform Gifts to Minor Act account (UGMA), where the parent serves as custodian until the child reaches age eighteen or twenty-one. Young people, influenced by popular culture, will purchase stocks because they are familiar with the brand, for example, Nike, Apple, and Sony. While these may be good investments, by purchasing individual stocks a teen is assuming more risk than necessary. The same upside potential is afforded via an index mutual fund but with substantially less risk than owning an individual stock.

If risk is ignored when it should be considered, what about taking advantage of situations when risk is low and the potential return is high. That is, do people buy low?

Unfortunately, the data shows the opposite. The Investment Company Institute, the trade group for the mutual fund industry, publishes data showing money flows into and out of mutual funds. During October 2008, when the prices of stocks were falling making them more attractive investments, there was a net outflow of money from mutual funds of approximately $70 billion, that is, people were selling low. Similarly, during the previous bear market of 2001 to 2002, there was a net outflow of $50 billion during June 2002, when stocks hit multi-year lows.[21]

Because teens were never taught about hindsight bias, that is, thinking a past trend will continue, this trait is often carried over into adult life, resulting in wealth destroying financial decisions.

Another example where wealth-destroying behavior resulted from not understanding the capitalist principle of risk vs. return occurred with an investment offered by Wall Street called "Auction Rate Securities" (ARS). These securities were marketed by brokers to individual investors as alternatives to CDs or savings accounts but with a higher rate of return. For the broker, it was an easy sell to offer greater return for no more risk, which is impossible if you understand that basic capitalistic principle. Instead of the rate being set by the bank, the rate was determined through an auction process whereby buyers of the securities would bid for the securities at different rates. Therefore, for the securities to be successfully sold, it required a successful auction, that is, buyers. In February 2008, the buyers for the ARS decided not to buy, thus, effectively freezing the market. Therefore, the thousands of investors who had previously purchased hundreds of millions of these securities with their retirement money found out in February 2008 that they could not get their money back—very different risk than a bank CD!

Here is what the Securities and Exchange Commission said in July 2009 in announcing its settlement with one of the brokers, TD Ameritrade:

> "TD Ameritrade improperly marketed ARS to retail customers as short-term investments without telling them about the special risks of the ARS market," said Donald M. Hoerl, Regional Director of the SEC's Denver Regional Office. "This settlement provides hundreds of millions of dollars to thousands of TD Ameritrade customers who hold ARS that are now illiquid."

While the press release stated that TD Ameritrade did not tell investors about the special risks of the ARS market, anyone understanding that basic capitalistic principal would have said to the broker, "How can I get the additional return without assuming greater risk; can you please explain to me the additional risk associated with auction rate securities?"

Chapter Eight

Does a Young Person Need Life Insurance?

No, not unless they are married or have dependents.

Simply, life insurance provides financial protection by paying money to a beneficiary upon the death of an insured. Unless the insured has dependents who look to him or her for food, clothing, education, or housing then there is no reason for a young person to purchase life insurance.

Many insurance agents, however, sell life insurance not as financial protection but as an investment opportunity. Not only are the investment attributes cited, but the tax advantaged investment growth within an insurance product, such as variable life insurance, is also cited as a selling point. Even Gerber, the baby food company, implores new parents to purchase life insurance from *their* life insurance subsidiary upon the birth of a child.

Therefore, young people have been convinced to purchase life insurance not only as the risk management tool it is intended to be, but also as a tax-deferred investment. Those insurance products that feature an investment component are whole, universal, and variable life policies, which when compared to a pure insurance product such as term life insurance carry higher premiums.

The problem is when a young person marries and has children, creating a real need for life insurance, they will tend to purchase more insurance from the same agent who sold the initial whole life or variable life policy. Because investment-oriented life insurance pays higher commissions than do term sales, which type of policy do you think the agent will recommend?

An understanding of the proper use of insurance will enable someone to understand that insurance and investment decisions are two separate items and that mixing the two, as is the case of investment-oriented life insurance, confuses the consumer, resulting in a poor purchase decision.

The saying "Buy the term and invest the rest," coined by A.J. Williams, an insurance entrepreneur who championed the use of term insurance, is a strong and powerful recommendation to keep your premium down by purchasing low-cost term insurance and take the difference and invest it separately.

What about Auto Insurance?

Teens and their parents are likely to face high premiums for insuring their first cars. Those premiums reflect higher accident rates for teen drivers. Since auto insurance is a risk management tool, young people need to ensure they have the proper coverage for the risks they incur when they drive.

The liability component of a personal auto policy (PAP) is the area teens should focus on.

This policy provision can be written as either "split" or "single limit" coverage. With split coverage, the policy may be 50/300/25, which means $50,000 bodily injury coverage per person, $300,000 bodily injury coverage for all persons in a single accident, and $25,000 property damage coverage emanating from an accident. A single limit policy, which results in lower out-of-pocket payments, might be $300,000, providing coverage in the aggregate for bodily injury and property damage from a single accident.

An example will illustrate the difference. Suppose a nineteen-year old has an accident causing $60,000 bodily injury (BI) to the other driver and $30,000 property damage (PD).

Split vs. Single Limit Auto Insurance		
Damages	**Split Limit Coverage**	**Single Limit**
$60,000 BI	$50,000 vs. $60M in damages	$60,000
$30,000 PD	$25,000 vs. $30M in damages	$30,000
Out-of-Pocket	$15,000	$0

The question then becomes why doesn't a teen, with a significantly higher probability of having an accident, have single limit coverage?

In a word…cost.

How much more is single limit coverage?

It is about 10 percent, perhaps 20 percent, more. Is it worth it?

If the premium for split limit coverage is $2,700 per year, single limit coverage would be about $3,240, an increase of $540/year.

Let's remember why insurance is purchased: to protect us in a worst-case scenario. Using the above example, the risk-reward for purchasing single limit coverage seems clear—pay an additional $540 and get back $15,000 (not having to pay the $15,000 out-of-pocket with split limit coverage); that's a good return on your investment!

What about Health Insurance?

While young people are a high-risk category when it comes to auto insurance, they are a low-risk category in terms of health insurance.

A low risk category means that young people are not intensive users of health insurance and, therefore, have more purchase options. One good option is a health savings account.

A health savings account combines a high-deductible catastrophic health insurance policy with a tax-deferred savings account. Such a combination offers young people advantages such as:

1. Lower premiums in return for high deductibles
2. Tax-deferred savings which carry forward, that is, are not lost if not spent
3. Flexibility in applying the health savings to treatments which might not be covered under a traditional health insurance plan, for example, skin care, dental braces, pregnancy screening

While a middle-aged person might have the need for lower deductibles because of frequent doctor/hospital visits, most young people are not in

that category. Indeed, one of the reasons behind the high-uninsured population is young people's refusal to buy health insurance because they think
they will never need it.

Other Forms of Insurance are Needed in Varying Degrees by Young People

Disability insurance, which covers payments received when an injury causes
a person not to be able to perform work, can be beneficial if young people
have high fixed costs. As a general rule, fixed costs, which include items
such as rent, mortgage payments, insurance premiums, and other items
should be covered by payments received under a disability policy.

Long-term care insurance, which pays for custodial care either in a nursing
home or at home, can be purchased, without significant premium increases,
when a person is approaching middle age, that is, beyond age forty.

Chapter Nine

How to Intelligently Use Financial Services

If young people and others understood how to use financial services properly, it would benefit not only them but also the country.

Consider:

1. An ability to calculate the effective interest rate or the rate actually earned on a CD would result in higher returns to consumers.
2. An understanding of how investment products are sold would result in lower commissions for brokers and better investments in young people's portfolios.
3. Knowing the difference between brokers who only offer a restricted group of mutual funds vs. those who offer a universal selection would result in superior returns compounded over numerous years, more wealth for the investor, and less for the mutual fund companies.
4. Understanding the purpose of life insurance would result in increased coverage at lower premiums.
5. Understanding a mortgage broker only gets paid if you purchase the loan might result in people being more wary of the mortgages being offered to them.
6. Knowledge that paying credit cards late or missing payments will damage your credit score and hinder your ability to get a job, and could quite possibly raise auto insurance premiums, might result in lower delinquency rates, lower losses, and ultimately lower rates for other young people who use credit cards.

The first experience many young people have using financial services will likely come from a bank. Therefore, one should understand how the banking system affects their use of bank products.

Banking: Deposit and Checking Services

Initially, the primary reason a teen will use a bank is to deposit and write checks from their account. Young people run into trouble because many write checks on uncollected funds resulting in a "bounced" check. This will certainly cause embarrassment and possibly result in a ding to their credit report. In addition, the bank, upon seeing a bounced check, will offer an overdraft line to prevent that from happening. Unfortunately, the overdraft line likely contains a high interest rate and it becomes addictive.

A better solution would be for young people to gain an understanding of how the financial system functions, specifically, how a check moves or "clears" through the Federal Reserve System. With this knowledge, young people would realize that a check written to pay a credit card company that maintains a lock box in close proximity would clear much faster than a check deposited into their account from a friend living across the country. While the banking system has recently moved to electronic clearing of checks, understanding the physical process of how a check moves from bank to bank, that is, "clears," provides a good foundation of how to use deposit and checking banking services.

How to Use a Credit Card

The next financial product a teen is likely to use is a credit card. This will be a card issued either in the teen's name alone or one co-signed by a parent, or simply another card issued through the parent's account. While sensible use of credit cards is discussed elsewhere in this book, the focus here is on the mechanics of operating a credit card account.

Young people must understand that cards operate on twenty-nine, thirty, or thirty-one-day billing cycles so that a bill received a few days after the billing cycle ends will reflect the activity during the previous billing cycle.

Unless the full amount from the previous cycle is paid, the remaining balance will be carried over into the next cycle, with interest charges added to the current cycle activity. Paying the minimum amount each month will not significantly reduce the principal, the loan will be outstanding for a long period, interest will be compounded over a higher principal (see Loan Amortization), and the total cost of the loan will increase.

An understanding of the difference between principal and interest, as well as what the monthly payment actually covers, is necessary to manage one's credit intelligently. Each month, the minimum required payment includes only a small portion of the principal with the majority of the payment going to the interest portion. In this fashion, the bank is able to maintain the loan as "current," that is, they don't have to reduce their profits by making a "provision" against the loan, and the principal balance remains high, providing a base for high future interest revenue (from the bank's perspective).

Using Loan Products

Continuing with bank services, a teen or young person is likely to use a loan from the government to pay for college, or a commercial loan from a bank to start a business, or buy a car. Loans from banks are offered on an amortizing basis, that is, the loan is repaid through periodic payments as compared to one-time "balloon" payment at the end. Elsewhere in this book, the concept of loan amortization has been explained. Apart from the specifics of how it works, it is important to realize that the longer the term of the loan, the lower the monthly payments, but the higher the overall cost of the loan because more interest will be paid over the loan's life. Loan amortizations also result in smaller amounts of principal being paid at the beginning of the loan. Therefore, if the loan is used to finance a car and the car is sold early in the loan, you could have a situation where more is owed on the loan than is the value of the car.

Moving from using a bank account to a brokerage account presents the young person with more complexities.

Brokerage Accounts

Who is a broker and what is a brokerage firm?

The first decision is where to open the brokerage account.

The first thing to understand is who or what is a "broker." A broker (discussed below) is an individual who sells products on behalf of his/her employer, that is, the "broker-dealer." A broker-dealer is a company that buys or sells securities for clients, the "broker" role, and buys and sells securities for its own account, the "dealer" role. You open a brokerage account at a broker-dealer firm.

Similar to the insurance protection provided by the Federal Deposit Insurance Corporation (FDIC) to bank depositors, the Securities Investor Protection Corporation (SIPC) provides insurance protection to clients of brokerage firms. SIPC insurance will protect the owners of brokerage accounts in the case of financial failure of the broker. For example, when Lehman Brothers declared bankruptcy in 2008, owners of brokerage accounts were entitled to receive payments from the SIPC for amounts in their accounts. The basic level of insurance protection is $100,000, covering the amount of cash in the brokerage account. However, each brokerage firm provides further levels of protection, so it is important to review each firm's policies before opening an account. It is important to remember that this insurance only pays if the brokerage firm fails; it does not cover losses incurred in an account because of stock market declines. This is important because a study conducted by the NASD (now FINRA) showed that 62 percent of respondents either thought or did not know that stock market losses were insured, which they are not.[22]

Should an account be open with a full service or discount brokerage firm?

The following should be considered when deciding which broker-dealer to use, that is, when opening an account:

Broker-Dealer Firms and Services				
	Full Range of Products	Commission Costs	Employs Own Brokers	Sells Own Products	SIPC Protection
Morgan Stanley, Merrill Lynch, and other "full service" brokerage firms	No, products restricted to those which pay fees to the brokerage firm	High for smaller accounts, discounted for larger accounts	Yes, work on commission and salary	Yes	Yes, limit depends upon firm's policy
Fidelity, Schwab, TD Ameritrade, these are known as the "independents"	Yes, all mutual funds offered as well as stocks, bonds and commodities	Moderate for most accounts, discounts offered for larger accounts	No, self directed or work through independent advisors	Yes and No	Yes, limit depends upon firm's policy
*E*Trade* and other online brokers	Yes	Low for most accounts	No, self directed	No	Yes, limit depends upon firm's policy

The basic purpose of opening a brokerage account is for the brokerage firm to execute trades for which a commission will be charged. Commission costs will range from $9 to $50 or more per trade for equities. Mutual fund trades may be commission free or up to $25 or more, depending on the platform. Full service brokers, who charge higher commissions, will also provide research, advice, and other services. Discount firms with lower commissions are "do-it-yourself," whereby you are on your own to make decisions. Buying and selling bonds does not carry an outright commission per se, but rather the broker will make a commission based upon the difference between the "bid" and "ask" price or the buy and sell prices for bonds they own or buy on your behalf.

Many "full service" brokerage firms have relationships with mutual fund companies. These relationships utilize a "revenue sharing" structure to compensate the brokerage firm for selling those mutual funds. It works this way; let us say a mutual fund company is desirous of getting its mutual funds on the "platform" of a particular brokerage firm; that is, the funds are approved for selling by the firm's brokers. In return for getting on the platform, the mutual fund company pays or "shares" part of the fees it earns on managing the fund with the brokerage firm. If the fund company charges the fund's investors (brokerage firm clients) 2 percent per year for managing the assets in the fund, they might agree to "share" 25 percent of the 2 percent.

On its face, this might seem reasonable except for the fact the brokerage firms tend to select funds where the "sharing fees" are the greatest; there simply are not enough fees to "share" in a low-cost index fund (see below). The data shows that funds with higher costs produce lower net returns. Specifically, equity mutual funds in the lowest cost quartile produced an average annual return of 13.8 percent, while those in the highest cost quartile produced an average annual return of 10.8 percent based on ten years of data through June 2001.[23] The difference was even more pronounced in the case of money market mutual funds where the low cost funds produced an annual return of 4.43 percent, while the high cost funds produced an annual return of 2.93 percent, a 51 percent difference in favor of the low cost fund. In a more recent study, it was found that domestic stock funds in the cheapest quintile had average annual returns of 3.35 percent during 2005 to March 2010, compared with average returns of 2.02 percent for funds in the most expensive quintile.[24]

If you are doing business with a full service firm, it is likely you will be paying for advice and recommendations. It is important to be knowledgeable of the regulatory framework in order to understand the type of advice or recommendations you may be offered. Employees of a brokerage firm who sell securities are known as registered representatives (registered reps) and they must have a Series 7 security license to sell products. This license allows them to charge a commission for selling a stock, bond, or mutual fund. This is different from a registered investment advisor (RIA) who usually works for an independent firm—independent in the sense the firm does not sell its own products. A registered investment advisor holds a Series 65 security license that entitles them to provide advice for a fee, but not to sell securities for a commission. FINRA regulates both the registered representative and the registered investment advisor. The rules governing the behavior of registered representatives and registered investment advisors are different and important from the perspective of you, the client. A registered representative has to abide by the "suitability" rule, which asks whether the investment being sold is "suitable" for the investor. Therefore, selling a risky emerging market equity fund to a conservative investor would not be suitable and would not be allowed. The primary rule governing the conduct of the registered investment advisor is the "fiduciary standard," meaning that at all times the RIA has to act as a fiduciary, putting the client's interest ahead of his/her own interest. This means that given the choice of two mutual funds that do the same thing, but one has lower costs, the RIA must select the lower cost fund.

Another difference is the way each is compensated. Registered reps earn commissions for selling products while RIA's charge fees based on a percentage of the assets managed. In reality, there is crossover in that some registered reps will charge fees in addition to commissions and some RIAs will take commissions for selling certain mutual funds (load funds) or annuities that carry high commission payments. A small percentage of RIAs are known as "fee only," meaning they take no commissions and only charge fees directly to the client.

Who will be the owner of the brokerage account?

Now that a brokerage firm has been selected, you must decide who will be the legal owner or how the account will be titled—in your name only, jointly with your spouse, as a UTMA account or a UGMA account with a teen as the beneficiary and the parent as the custodian. If one person is the owner, it is an "individual" account. If a husband and wife are joint owners, it is a "joint" account. In a joint account, if one party dies the other party becomes the sole owner of the assets in the account. UTMA or UGMA accounts are custodial accounts, whereby parents serve as the custodian, making decisions about the account until the child reaches the age of eighteen or twenty-one in certain states, at which time the child becomes the account holder with decision-making authority. Unearned income (investment income, see below) earned in UTMA or UGMAs that is less than an inflation-adjusted annual amount, currently $1,900, is taxed at the child's rate; above that, any income earned will be taxed at the parent's tax rate.

Funding a brokerage account

How will the account initially be funded? If a check is being written, it should be made out to the name of the firm, for example, "Fidelity Investments," with the account number written on the bottom left. If a wire transfer (electronic movement of funds) is to be made, then you must provide the bank sending the wire (sending the money) with the ABA# for the receiving bank used by the brokerage firm, the "for Further Credit" account number, and finally your account number at the brokerage firm.

Money Transfer Identifiers	
ABA#	identifies the brokerage firm's bank
For Further Credit	identifies the account number of the brokerage firm at the bank
Final Account Number	the account number of your brokerage account at the firm

ABA numbers, which are the American Banking Association routing numbers, are assigned to banks as their identifying code so that money can be "routed" from bank to bank. Most money that is transferred between people or between companies is transferred electronically through one of two ways:

1. Wire transfers
2. ACH transfers

Wire transfers, usually for larger dollar amounts, are processed directly from bank to bank. Each bank has an ABA identifying code and the wire is processed through the Federal Reserve Wire Network. If the wire is requested prior to 3:00 PM Eastern Standard Time, the funds will arrive in the account on the same day. There is a charge for using the Federal Reserve Wire Network; depending on your bank, it can be between $15 and $30.

ACH transfers are used to handle smaller transactions. ACH stands for "Automated Check Handling" and involves the processing of electronic checks through the banking network. ACH transactions are processed in the same manner as paper checks but without the paper. To understand let's see how a typical paper check is processed.

First, some terms:

Clear a check – the process by which money is transferred from your bank account to the bank account of the company or the person to whom you have written the check.

Federal Reserve Clearing System – a network of twelve Federal Reserve Districts and Federal Reserve Bank branches within each district around the country. Each bank in the U.S. that is a member of the Federal Reserve System, clears checks through its Federal Reserve

District branch bank. Prior to 2004, when the "Check 21" system began, banks cleared paper checks for processing by sending the paper check to their local Federal Reserve branch bank. With the advent of Check 21, rather than sending the paper check, banks use electronic images and transmit the information electronically.

Federal Reserve Banks and Districts

Federal Reserve District Banks:

Federal Reserve District	Federal Reserve Bank
1	Boston
2	New York
3	Philadelphia
4	Cleveland
5	Richmond
6	Atlanta
7	Chicago
8	St. Louis
9	Minneapolis
10	Kansas City
11	Dallas
12	San Francisco

Each district also has branch cities; for example, the Federal Reserve District number five, located in Richmond, has branch cities in Baltimore and Charlotte. The branch cities are used by banks in the district to clear checks, as shown in the diagram below.

How a Paper Check Clears through the Banking System

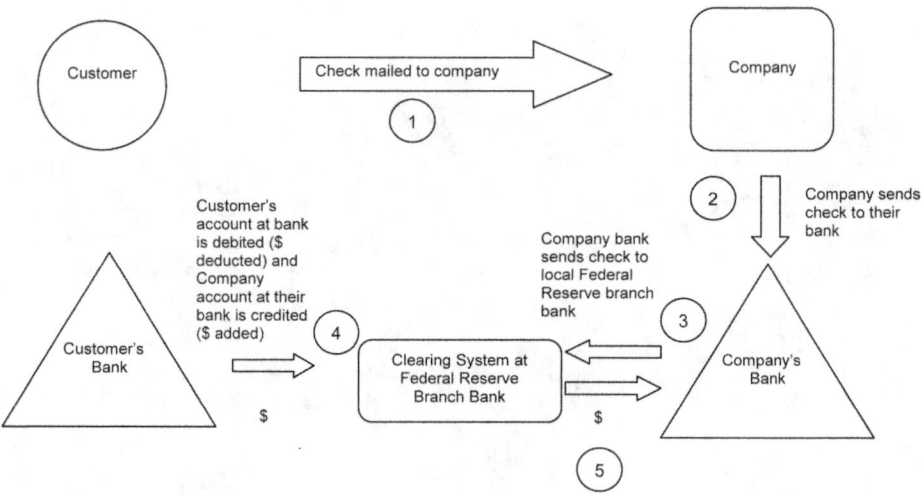

An ACH transfer does this all electronically through an electronic clearinghouse, which is a computer system operated by the banks. Electronically, dollars are added to the account of the company's bank and are subtracted from the account of the customer's bank. As compared to a wire transfer, this can take up to two to three days and will generally not involve a charge.

How is trading done in a brokerage account?

Once the money is in the brokerage account, you must be aware of the following prior to making a trade:

If you want to buy a stock, say Apple Computer, Inc., you will first have to know the "ticker" symbol for Apple, which happens to be "AAPL." If you wanted to purchase IBM Corporation, its ticker symbol is "IBM." All stocks that trade through the NASDAQ (National Association of Securities Dealers Automated Quotations Systems) have four letters as the symbol, while those that trade on the New York Stock Exchange (NYSE) have one, two, or three letters as their symbol.

In the U.S., the two main stock exchanges are the NASDAQ and the NYSE. The NASDAQ is a computer network linking broker-dealers; therefore, the NASDAQ does not physically exist—think of it as stock trading through the Internet. The NYSE, on the other hand, is housed in a building on Wall Street in New York City; it is sometimes referred to as the "Big Board." As compared to the NASDAQ, brokers make trades with one another, through a "specialist," on the floor of the NYSE. The NYSE "specialist" system assigns each stock listed for trading on the NYSE to a specialist firm. Each of those firms is responsible for making a continuous, always on, market for those stocks during the trading day, which lasts from 9:30 AM to 4:00 PM Eastern Standard Time.

Making a market in a stock means offering to buy or sell the stock at any time. An offer to buy a stock is called the *bid* price and the offer to sell the stock is called the *ask* price. The specialist makes these prices based upon the prices of the previous trade and usually in increments of 1/8 of a dollar or $0.125. Therefore, if the last trade for IBM, Inc., was at $137 then the specialist would offer to buy IBM at $136.875 ($137 − $0.125) and offer to sell IBM at $137.125 ($137 +$0.125).

Suppose you have a brokerage account at Merrill Lynch and you want to buy fifty shares of IBM. You instruct your local broker at Merrill Lynch to purchase the fifty shares. Your local Merrill broker will instruct their floor broker—the Merrill Lynch broker on the floor of the NYSE—to approach the specialist who handles IBM. The specialist offers to sell IBM at $137.125 and the Merrill floor broker agrees to buy the fifty shares. The order is transmitted back to your local Merrill broker and the trade is executed in your account.

For the trade to settle (cash is added and stock subtracted from your account if you sell, or cash is deducted and stock is added to your account if you buy) two things have to happen:

1. You must have at least $6,906.25 in cash in your account to cover the purchase of the shares and the $50 commission charged by Merrill ($137.125 x 50 + $50)
2. Time: three days have to pass

Suppose you instructed Merrill to purchase these IBM shares on Monday. Because of the time required to process the trades through the stock exchange, the trade will not *settle* (that is, the money deducted from your cash and the shares added to your account) until Thursday. In other words, stocks have a three-day settlement period.

If instead you wanted to purchase AAPL, your Merrill broker, rather than contacting the Merrill NYSE floor broker, would put the trade into the NASDAQ computer system. He or she has a computer screen that shows prices for which other brokers will sell or buy APPL. He tells you the price and if you agree, the trade is executed in your account with the same three-day settlement period as with trades executed on the NYSE.

If you instead decided to purchase a mutual fund, the settlement period will only take one day—cash is deducted and the shares of the mutual fund are added to your account on the next day. Open-ended mutual fund shares are purchased directly from the mutual fund company that manages the fund. An open-ended mutual fund is one that continuously issues new shares when someone wants to purchase. A closed-end mutual fund has a pre-determined number of shares, and those shares are traded on the NYSE or the American Stock Exchange or AMEX. The AMEX operates in the same way as the NYSE, using floor brokers to trade among themselves, but does not use the specialist system of the NYSE.

Understanding How Financial Products and Services Are Sold

Knowledge of how financial services are sold would create a consumer better able to sift through the advertisements and sales pitches used to sell many financial products.

What is a mutual fund?

Let's examine mutual funds.

The first thing to understand about mutual funds is that a mutual fund is a company, and like any company, it needs to cover its expenses in order to operate. Therefore, similar to other companies, mutual funds charge their shareholders fees to run the company.

The second thing to know is that studies have found that there exists an inverse relationship between the fees a fund company charges and the returns it produces for its shareholders.

The amount of fees a fund company charges is disclosed in its *prospectus*. The prospectus is a document a company has to prepare and file with the *Securities and Exchange Commission* or SEC in order to sell securities to the public. The SEC is the governmental agency that regulates the sales of shares to the investing public. The SEC will review the prospectus to see whether all the required information has been included. However, it is important to realize that when the SEC grants its approval to the company to sell its shares, it is only saying that all the required information has been included within the prospectus, not that buying the shares represents a good investment. At times, some brokers will say that the "shares have been approved by the SEC" to try to convince you it is a good investment. This is a false and unlawful claim for any broker to make.

Within the prospectus, the company will report the level of expenses for the last year, along with the total assets of the company. The total assets of a mutual fund company represent the amount of money individuals have invested in the fund. Also disclosed is something called the *expense ratio*, which is calculated by taking the company's annual expenses and dividing by the average amount of assets in the fund over the past year.

What are the expenses of a mutual fund company?

- *Management Fees*: These are the fees charged to manage the assets of the fund. Managing the assets of a fund entails doing research on different companies to investigate their sales growth, profit margins, and outlook for the future. There are additional costs for traveling to meet with the company's management and talk to competitors and suppliers—all focused on trying to find companies whose shares will rise more rapidly than the overall stock market.

- *Trading Costs*: Each and every time the fund makes a trade they have to pay trading commissions; these costs are passed on to the fund's shareholders, that is, the investors—people like you.

- *Advertising*: If you pick up a newspaper, watch financial oriented television, or listen to financial radio shows, you will often read, see, or hear advertisements for mutual fund companies. Once again, these costs are passed on to the company's shareholders, who are the fund investors.

- *Distribution Costs*: Many funds make payments to brokerage firms and 401(k) plans (see more below) to "accept" their funds onto their platforms; also known as *revenue sharing*, these costs are passed on to the firm's shareholders and paid by you.

In addition to the operating expenses listed above, sometimes a fund will have to sell some investments in order to raise cash to pay people who want to withdraw their money from the fund. Such sales may trigger taxes in the form of *capital gains taxes* levied against investments sold at a price higher than what they were purchased for. Even if you did not sell your shares in the fund, these taxes are passed on to all fund owners and you will get a tax bill at the end of the year for your portion of these taxes. Funds which trade frequently tend to generate "unwanted" (in the sense you did not generate the gain by a sale of your position, instead you paid a portion of the tax from the sale of someone else's position) capital gains. Therefore, a smart investor tends to avoid funds with excessive trading, also known as high "turnover."

Third, young people should know that funds with higher expenses are those that spend a lot of money trying to find the "right" stocks to buy; they will have high management fees, research, traveling, and trading costs as noted above. Other funds, known as *index* funds, rather than trying to find the five or ten "best" stocks, buy all the stocks within a pre-defined group or index. Because it is very difficult to find those stocks that will increase more than the overall market, they do not spend money to try to do what is difficult or impossible. Studies have shown that, over periods of time—five, ten, or fifteen years—index funds produce a higher return than most funds that actively try and beat the market; these funds, by the way, are known as *actively managed funds*.

Fourth, financial professionals who work at the large brokerage firms, Morgan Stanley, Merrill Lynch, and so on, will more often than not offer you those funds that pay them money to sell. As noted above, registered reps earn substantial compensation from commissions generated by fund sales; therefore, it is likely they will only offer those funds that pay them the highest commission. As is becoming obvious, these funds are not necessarily the best for their client.

In addition to the up-front money brokers get from selling funds, they also receive an on-going payment from you as long as you own the fund.

These payments, unknown to most fund investors, are known as 12b - 1 fees and are part of the "revenue sharing" referred to above; they are buried within the expenses of the fund, but by law, they are disclosed in the fund's prospectus.

Teens and young people need to understand that, many times, their broker will state there is no cost for managing their account, that all trades are commission free though you continue to pay (through the 12b - 1 fee) unknowingly because this fee is not disclosed. Not only is this fee not disclosed, it is also hard to locate where the fee is charged. When you get your monthly statement or a performance report of returns, you will not see the fee because it is charged prior to calculating the return on your mutual funds—you never see it!

Using a 401 (k) Plan

Teens and young adults entering their first job will likely have a conversation with their human resource manager about something very confusing or of little interest—the company's retirement benefit program, or most likely, the 401(k) plan.

When our parents and grandparents had a pension, it was likely called a *defined benefit* pension plan. Today, most companies have switched to *defined contribution* plans; a 401(k) is a type of defined contribution pension plan.

Defined benefit refers to an amount of money a company will pay a worker when he or she retires in some relation to their salary and the amount of time they have worked there; that is, the employee receives a fixed monthly payment or "benefit" from the date of retirement until death. Under a defined benefit plan, the company has the obligation to make the investment decisions and to make the retirement benefit payments.

Defined contribution refers to a pension plan where an amount of money, the "contribution," is set aside for the employee through a combination of salary deductions and employer matching contributions. However, in contrast to a defined benefit plan where the employer makes the investment decisions and guarantees the retirement benefit, the employee has to make the investment decisions to produce the income to be received in retirement.

A pension plan is a program through which payments are made into a fund, managed by either the company (defined benefit) or the employee (defined contribution), in order to provide income to an employee once they retire or no longer work.

Why should a teen or young adult care about a 401(k)?

When you retire, you will need income in order to buy the things you need and want, such as:

- Food
- Clothing
- Music
- Cars
- TVs and computers
- Mortgage/rent

As you get older, you might also have health problems that will require you to make out-of-pocket payments. *Out-of-pocket* payments refer to those costs not covered by your health insurance that you must pay.

Today many people decide to retire when they are sixty-two or sixty-six, some earlier and some later. When you retire, you are no longer working; therefore, you receive no salary. Because of increased life expectancy, you might very well live until ninety or longer! Therefore, you need to plan for a thirty or forty-year retirement, meaning your pension must be sufficient to cover your costs for as long as you live.

Young people need to pay attention to their 401(k), because the earlier you start participating in the plan, the more money you will have when you decide to retire. By participating in the plan as early as possible, you also decrease the possibility of losing money in the stock market. Without getting into the technical details, the point is that the longer you have to invest your money, the lower the possibility of losing money. That is, you have a much greater probability of losing money over a five rather than a fifteen or thirty year period. Give yourself a leg up and start early to finish with more money when you retire!

How you manage your 401(k) also affects the financial stability of the country. In isolation, your actions will have no impact, but your actions, if emulated by millions of people like you, will have a big impact. If you act in a certain manner, there is a strong likelihood that others with your background, education, and position are also doing the same. Furthermore, things you learn early on are carried forward into adult life, unless some type of corrective action is taken.

What type of behavior regarding 401(k) plans on the part of young adults and others has contributed to financial instability in the country?

- Making investments in rapidly rising stocks or mutual funds, assuming what happened in the past will again happen in the future, for example, tech stocks in 1999 to 2000, emerging market stocks in 2005 to 2006, real estate oriented stocks in 2004 to 2007.

- Investing in your company's shares based upon the belief that since you work there it must be a great investment. This "self dealing" on the part of companies—for example, sometimes the matching contribution given by the employer is in the form of company stock—bids up the company's stock price to unsustainable levels, causing greater volatility or risk in the stock market.

In all likelihood, you will continue to make these mistakes as an adult, because unless you seek the knowledge required to manage your money like a professional, you will not learn the necessary skills to avoid these mistakes. Furthermore, in all likelihood, you will not be a prime prospect for a professional investment advisor who possesses the necessary skills and credentials. The average 401(k) balance is about $40,000 and that amount of money will not attract many investment advisors to your door to offer professional advice.

This has serious implications for the country as a whole because when you multiply all those $40,000 accounts by their aggregate numbers, you get a very large amount of money, which, in essence, is not being professionally managed, but is being moved around by people lacking the knowledge of how to do so. To quantify this: a survey of 401(k) plan participants determined there were twenty-two million participants in these plans at the end of 2008.[25] If the average balance was approximately $40,000, then 401(k) accounts totaled approximately $880 billion, or roughly one-tenth of the value of all traded equities in the U.S. This represents a large amount of retirement funds that are not professionally managed and could, therefore, cause damage (as noted above) to the U.S. equity markets and individual retirement wealth by chasing returns (buying high) and selling low.

Check Cashing Services

Many teens and young adults do not use a bank or have a bank account and, therefore, rely on the services of check cashing stores to cash paychecks.

Once again, lack of knowledge is costly for the individual and detrimental for the economy.

If someone does not understand the difference between an annual percentage rate and an effective annual rate, they will be deceived by the stated rate vs. what they are actually paying. This results in less wealth to the individual, forcing them to borrow more— probably from a high interest credit card—which sadly, ultimately, results in higher debt write-offs for card issuers. When this happens, we all bear the burden in terms of higher credit card rates.

Suppose Joe walks into the check-cashing store and sees a sign:

10% Compounded Monthly

He probably thinks 10 percent is a reasonable interest rate and gladly accepts the advance against his future paycheck.

This rate, however, translates into:

$$\text{Effective Annual Rate} = (1 + .10/12)^{12} - 1 = 10.5\%$$

If Joe received an advance of $1,000, he would owe $1,105 at the end of the year, which would be deducted from his paycheck pushing him into what I call the "confused debt cycle." Multiply Joe's action by the hundreds of thousands, if not millions, who use check cashing services and the damage to the economy becomes clear.

"Confused Debt Cycle"

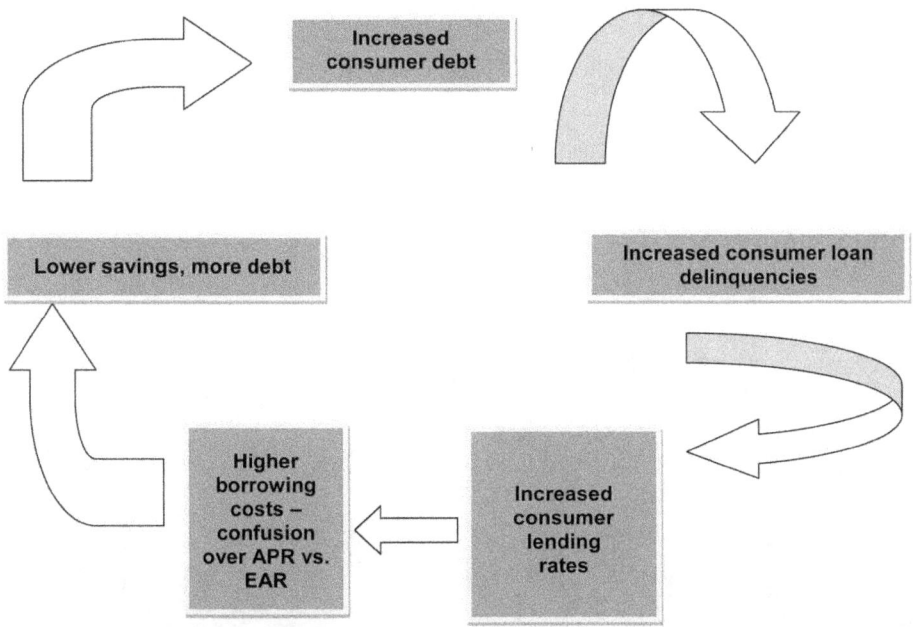

Increased consumer debt

Increased consumer loan delinquencies

Increased consumer lending rates

Higher borrowing costs – confusion over APR vs. EAR

Lower savings, more debt

Chapter Ten

WHAT A YOUNG PERSON NEEDS TO UNDERSTAND ABOUT
THE U.S. TAX SYSTEM

Let's face it, most young people, upon receiving their first paycheck, don't fully understand where their money goes to account for the difference between their gross and net pay; I didn't and I had a M.B.A.!

When told it has to do with taxes, they then become interested in learning about taxes.

I remember on my first job the explanation given to me about income and payroll taxes, health care, and other deductions; I did not care nor did I quite understand!

Young people do care that money is being deducted from their paycheck; they are just not that interested that some of it has to do with their retirement, which is something fifty years down the road!

What Does a Teen Need to Know about the U.S. Tax System, and How Would This Knowledge Improve Their Finances and the Country as a Whole?

The first thing to understand is that there are two types of taxes deducted from a paycheck:

1. *Income Tax*: The amount paid to the federal government is based upon one of five (as of 2010) income brackets (see below) with a higher tax rate percent for higher income brackets. In every state except Alaska, Washington, South Dakota, Wyoming, Texas, Florida, and Nevada state income taxes are also deducted with each

state setting their own rates. Certain cities also charge an income tax to residents and people who work there.

2. *Payroll Tax*: This is a fixed percent of your salary, 6.2 percent for Social Security and 1.45 percent for Medicare or 7.65 percent in total, paid up to a salary of $106,800; therefore, the maximum amount of payroll tax taken out of the paycheck is $8,170 under current law.

Generally, income tax is used by the federal government in Washington, D.C., to pay for the costs of running the government and is collected by "withholding" a percentage of your salary when you are paid. The payroll tax represents your contribution to your Social Security and Medicare accounts; your employer will also pay an equal amount into your account. Social Security entitles you to receive an amount of money monthly, beginning, depending upon when you were born, when you are sixty-two, sixty-six, or older for the rest of your life.

The six federal income tax brackets for 2010 are:

Income Tax Brackets 2010 Single Filer				
Taxable Income ($)	Base Tax ($)	Plus	Rate on Excess (%)	Of the Amount Over ($)
0 to 8,375	0	+	10	0
8,376 to 34,000	837.5	+	15	8,376
34,001 to 82,400	4,681	+	25	34,000
82,401 to 171,850	16,781	+	28	82,400
171,851 to 373,650	41,827	+	33	171,850
Over 373,651	108,421	+	35	373,650

Suppose your salary is $36,700, how much income tax will you pay?

Your salary puts you in the 25 percent bracket:

Tax Calculation for the 25% Bracket:

Base Tax	=		$4,681
Excess	=	($36,700-$34,001) x .25	+ $675
		Total Tax	$5,355.8

Being in the 25 percent bracket means that your "marginal," or last dollar, earned is being taxed at a rate of 25 percent.

How much payroll tax will be deducted from your paycheck?

$$\$36,700 \text{ x } .0765 \quad = \quad \$2,807.5$$

Assuming you are paid on a bi-weekly basis (once every two weeks) then one of your twenty-six paychecks might look like this:

Take-Home Pay Calculation:

Gross Salary	$1,412
Federal withholding	$206 (income tax @ 25% rate bracket)
FICA	$108 (Social Security + Medicare)
Net Salary	$1,098

"FICA" stands for Federal Insurance Contributions Act. Of the $108.00, $87.50 goes to your Social Security account and $20.50 goes to your Medicare contribution. Medicare is the government run insurance program that pays part of your health insurance when you turn sixty-five, while Medicaid is a federal program to help people, who earn below a certain level, purchase health insurance.

While you have had tax taken from your paycheck, called *withholding*, this may not be the final amount of tax you owe; in fact, you might owe less or more.

Whether you owe more or less is determined when you file your tax return, or the 1040 form. Form 1040 is what you file to either recover or add to the amount of tax that was already taken out of your paycheck, that is, the withholding.

Tax Deductions – 1040 Form

On the 1040 form, there are two types of deductions: *above-the-line* and *below-the-line*. Deductions are expenses you have paid that reduce the amount of your *taxable income,* which is the income on which your tax is calculated.

For example, many deductions will reduce your taxable income; therefore, your actual tax, when calculated on the 1040 form, may turn out to be less than the amount that was already withdrawn from your paycheck; in that case, you will get a refund.

Alternatively, you may have received income for which you have not paid tax; for example, you have a part-time job as a waitress, for which you have received tips and no tax has been taken out. Because this is income to you, it must be reported on the 1040 form; in this case, after calculating your tax, your final *tax liability* may be higher than the amount that was taken out of your paycheck, in which case you will owe money.

What are the two types of deductions?

"Above-the-line" deductions are those reported directly on the first page of the 1040 form and are used to determine your *adjusted gross income* (AGI); they include items such as:

Above-the-Line Tax Deductions:

- Contributions to an Individual Retirement Account (IRA)
- Tuition for attending night school, online schools, or any other education expenses which you pay for yourself
- Interest on student loans
- Contributions to Health Savings Accounts
- Moving expenses incurred to take a new job

There are others, but these are the most common ones young adults will incur. An individual's AGI is an important figure because it affects the ability to use "below-the- line" deductions. For example, certain deductions are not allowed if the AGI is too high, that is, the IRA deduction if you or your spouse participate in a 401(k) plan and itemized deductions in aggregate will be curtailed.

"Below-the-line" deductions are those that are referred to as *itemized deductions* and are reported on schedule A of the 1040 form. These deductions are subtracted from your AGI to determine your *taxable income*. Itemized deductions include items such as:

Below-the-Line Tax Deductions:

- State income taxes and local property taxes
- Interest on mortgages
- Expenses you incur for your job that are not reimbursed by your employer
- Medical expenses which you pay out of pocket, if they exceed 7.5 percent of your AGI
- Miscellaneous expenses in excess of 2.5 percent of your AGI

Therefore, a good tax management strategy is to manage your AGI down by making contributions to an IRA and/or a Health Savings Account. See the next chapter regarding saving for retirement.

The lower your AGI, the easier it is to take deductions for medical expenses. In addition, other deductions are tied to AGI, such that if your AGI is too high, the amount of the deduction is reduced or eliminated.

Because certain expenses reduce your taxable income and, therefore, the amount of taxes paid, the true cost of these expenses must be viewed on an "after-tax basis," which is the actual cost, less the tax savings resulting from the expense. For example, suppose you have $2,500 in tuition expenses for an online class you are taking and that you are in the 25 percent tax bracket.

The actual out-of-pocket cost to you is less than $2,500:

After-tax Cost of a Tax-deductible Expense:

Gross tuition expense:	$2,500
Reduction in taxes because tuition expense is tax-deductible:	$2,500 x .25 = $625
After-tax cost of tuition expense	$1,875

The after-tax cost of any item is calculated as: cost of item (1-tax rate).

Apart from deductions, which reduce your taxable income, there are *tax credits* that, dollar-for-dollar, directly reduce your tax liability. Therefore, an important tax planning point is that tax deductions indirectly reduce your tax liability by reducing taxable income, while tax credits directly reduce your taxes by reducing your tax liability.

There are two types of tax credits, *refundable* and *non-refundable*. Refundable credits are paid to you even if they are greater than your tax liability, while non-refundable credits are available to only reduce your tax liability with no additional refund beyond that.

Tax credits work as follows:

Using our above example, your salary is $36,700, you make a $5,000 contribution to an IRA, you have $1,500 in medical expenses, and you have two children.

How a Refundable Tax Credit Works:

Gross Income	$36,700
Above the line deduction/IRA	-$5,000
Adjusted Gross Income	$31,700
Below the line deduction/Medical	-$1,500
Taxable Income	$30,200
Tax liability from rate table	$4,111
Earned Income Tax Credit	$4,824

The U.S. government sends you a check for $713 and you owe no taxes.

Now assume your salary is $25,000, you make a $4,000 contribution to an IRA, your medical expense is $3,500, you have $5,000 in student loan interest, and you have $2,500 of unreimbursed business expenses.

Example of a non-refundable tax credit:

How a Non-Refundable Tax Credit Works:

Gross Income	$25,000
Above the line deduction/IRA	-$4,000
Above the line deduction/Interest	-$5,000
Adjusted Gross Income	$16,000
Below the line deduction/Medical	-$3,500
Below the line deduction/Unreimbursed	-$2,500
Taxable Income	$10,000
Tax liability from rate table	$1,081

Child Tax Credit $2,000 available, $1,081 amount of non-refundable child tax credit applied

Though $2,000 of the child tax credit was potentially available, only $1,081 could be used, as your tax liability was less than the credit; you now owe no taxes to the U.S. government.

Another item young people need be aware of is their *filing status*, which refers to the type of tax return filed:

> ### Tax-filing Status Categories:
>
> - Single
> - Married filing jointly
> - Head of household
> - Married filing separately

If you are married, you will want to file using the "Married Filing Jointly" category because it results in lower tax liability than if each spouse files separately as "Single." If one of the spouses is a "nonresident alien" or a person residing in the U.S. but not a citizen, you cannot file as Married Filing Jointly.

If you are not married, or legally separated from your spouse under a divorce decree or married but living apart from your spouse for the last six months of the tax year and you have a child or another person for whom you can claim as a *dependent*, it is best to file as "Head of Household," which will result in lower tax liability than if each spouse filed as a "Single." However, the tax liability will be higher than if a return was filed as Married Filing Jointly.

When do you need to pay your taxes?

Your taxes are due by April 15 of the following year; for example, taxes for the calendar year 2009 were due by April 15, 2010. Extensions to file the return are available for six months, such that the 1040 form must be filed by October 15, 2010. To obtain an extension, file the 4868 form or file through an e-file extension request. Even though you may file your tax return late, any tax must be paid by the regular due date, April 15 to avoid interest and penalties.

An understanding of the proper use of tax deductions and credits, which would result in greater tax savings to individuals, might result in increased compliance (greater willingness to declare income) and more revenues to the government.

Chapter Eleven

RETIREMENT INCOME – WHY SHOULD A YOUNG PERSON CARE?

Question: How do I gain an additional $162,272 over thirty years?
Answer: By investing in a tax-deferred account vs. a taxable account.

This assumes a thirty-year investment period, beginning with nothing, contributing $4,000 per year for thirty years, and earning 7 percent per year in an IRA, and 5 percent after-tax per year in a taxable account.

An Individual Retirement Account (IRA) is a *tax-deferred* account, meaning taxes are not owed until money is withdrawn from the IRA.

Question: How do I get a tax deduction each time I make an investment?
Answer: By investing each year into an IRA.

When you stop working, you will no longer receive a salary; therefore, you must accumulate enough money while you are working in order to have the money you need once you retire.

One of the ways to do that is by contributing annually to an IRA. As shown below, tax-deferred investing is the best way to increase your money over time.

To be successful, you must start contributing while you are young and do it consistently throughout your working life.

To demonstrate the importance of contributing to an IRA and other retirement savings, consider the results of the "2007 Retirement Confidence Survey" conducted by the Employee Benefit Research Institute.

Seventy-three percent of the money you will spend when you no longer have a salary will come from your personal savings!

Sources of Retirement Income

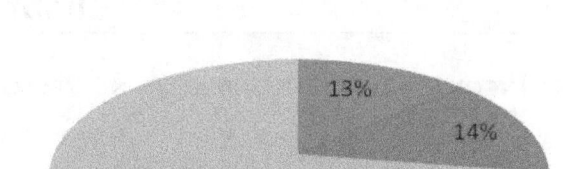

Not only will most of the money you spend come from your savings, but it will also have to last a long time. If you retire when you are sixty-five, the number of years you may have to live off your savings is shown below:

Life Expectancy Probabilities[26]		
	Probability	Age
Male	75%	78
	50%	85
Female	75%	81
	50%	88

Therefore, if you stop working when you are sixty-five and are a female, it is highly likely you will live another sixteen years, and quite possible another twenty-three years; your money has to last this long!

How will you possibly save enough money?

Tax Deferred Investing

You have two major things working in your favor:

1. By starting young, you have time on your side and time maximizes the benefit of *compounding*, which is discussed below.
2. The government provides ways for you to invest such that should the investment increase in value, it will not be taxed; this is known as *tax-deferred investing*; not taxing your investment earnings until you withdraw the money is the fastest way your money can grow.

There are various tax-deferred investments for retirement and they include:

- IRA
- Roth IRA
- 401(k) plan
- 457 plan
- 403(b) plan
- Keogh plan
- Self Employment Plan or SEP

There are others, but these are the main ones. Let's see how they work.

As previously noted, an *IRA* or Individual Retirement Account is an account you establish and contribute to yearly. Most IRA accounts are opened at a brokerage firm, though some banks also offer these accounts. In addition, these accounts can also be opened directly at mutual fund companies, such as Vanguard or Fidelity. The contributions you make are above-the-line tax deductions to your income. The money grows tax-free while inside the account. When you withdraw the funds, you will pay tax on the amount withdrawn.

A *Roth IRA* is a variation of the traditional IRA with the difference being there is no tax deduction for the annual amount you contribute. Once the money is inside the account, like the traditional IRA, it will grow tax-free. Another difference is when you withdraw money, unlike a traditional IRA, you will not be taxed on the amount withdrawn. Not everyone can have a Roth IRA, because if your AGI is above certain levels you will not be eligible to set up a Roth IRA. Therefore, a good tax planning strategy is to establish a Roth IRA before you get a raise, which might disqualify you!

If you work for a company, it is likely some type of retirement plan will be offered, and it will probably be something called a *401(k)*. As noted elsewhere, in a 401(k) plan, you direct your employer to deduct a percentage of your salary, say 6 percent, and deposit this into your account within the company 401(k) plan. Some employers go a step further and "match" a portion of the amount you contribute with their money. In this sense, the *employer match* represents "free" money to you. Similar to an IRA, the money in your 401(k) account will grow tax free, but you will be taxed on it when you withdraw the funds. The company that offers the 401(k), your employer, is called the *plan sponsor*. You may not withdraw money from your account, without a 10 percent penalty, until you are older than fifty-nine-and-a-half years old, though you may be able to borrow against it. If you leave the company and take another job, you can *rollover* the money in your account into the 401(k) plan at your new employer or you can roll it over, into a *Rollover IRA*. A Rollover IRA functions just as a traditional IRA except that it is funded with money from a 401(k) plan rather than annual contributions. Once the Rollover IRA is established, you can make annual contributions into it going forward.

If you are a member of a union or a teacher, you will have access to either a *457* or a *403(b)* plan, which are similar to 401(k) plans. Because many teachers have defined benefit plans from the states in which they work, the 403(b) plan is viewed as a supplemental plan to their main pension. Local school boards, who administer the 403(b) plans, do not make matching contributions.

If you work for yourself, you can set up a Self Employment Pension or *SEP*. A SEP is similar to an IRA in that you make pre-tax contributions, the money is not taxed while in the SEP, and you are taxed when you make withdrawals. Compared to an IRA a SEP allows you to make larger contributions; the amount you are permitted to contribute is based upon the income generated in your business.

All of the previously described tax-deferred savings plans have the following features in common:

- Except for certain exceptions, if you withdraw money prior to age fifty-nine-and-a-half, you will incur a 10 percent penalty.

- Except for the Roth IRA, you must begin withdrawals at age seventy-and-a-half on which you will be taxed at your ordinary income tax rate determined according to the tax rate brackets.

- The only plan that permits borrowing is a 401(k).

Compounding

The other advantage of increased savings early in life is the time young people have to maximize the benefits of *compounding*. Compounding is earning interest on interest, and as you increase the number of years for which compounding occurs, the money grows exponentially.

Consider an example where you save $3,000 per year and earn 5 percent per year. How much will you accumulate at the end of five, ten, fifteen, twenty, and thirty years?

How Compounding Works	
Investment Period	**Money Accumulated ($)**
5 years	16,576
10 years	37,733
15 years	64,735
20 years	99,197
30 years	199,316

The effects of compounding are apparent; earning a return on your investment earnings from the previous year, and doing this many times, results in large increases in your money!

Furthermore, when you do this within one of the tax-deferred retirement plans mentioned above, so as to not to pay taxes on the year-to-year earnings, your money increases even more.

An important consideration with the above mentioned savings plans is that they all require choosing the investments inside the plan, which distinguishes these plans from defined benefit plans where the employer chooses the investments.

Defined Benefit Plans

Another type of savings plan that pays you money when you stop working is called a defined benefit plan, otherwise known as a traditional pension plan. In these plans, similar to a 401(k), your employer deducts part of your salary; however, rather than giving the money to you to invest, they use it to make investments that will be used, when you retire, to pay you money each month for the rest of your life. That's the reason they are called defined benefit, in that the benefit, or the money to be paid to you when you stop working, is defined or stated. It is then the obligation of the company to ensure they have the money to pay you. Even if the investments made on your behalf do not produce enough to pay your monthly pension, the company is still required to pay the monthly benefit.

In this way, many regard this type of pension plan as superior since there is a guaranty of the monthly payment. Of course, this guaranty is only as good as the company providing it. There are some safeguards, however, in that the government created the Pension Benefit Guaranty Corporation (PBGC), which makes payments to employees in the case of their company being *bankrupt* and not being able to pay the pension.

In the past, most pensions provided were of this type. Over the past twenty years, however, many companies have moved away from defined benefit pensions and instituted defined contribution plans; a 401(k) is a defined contribution plan because rather than the benefit defined to you, the contribution is, and it is up to you to select the investments and create your own benefit!

Chapter Twelve

As a teen or young person, you are allowed, even encouraged, to make riskier investments than your parents are.

The reason is one of the principles of capitalism—to get more return you need to take more risk.

Risk is good.

Question: Can you take the risk?
Answer: Yes, if you are on the short side of thirty years of age!

What Is Risk?

Possibility of losing money? Not exactly.

In investing, risk is simply the daily ups and downs of an investment, that is, the bumps in the road. Only those investments that have large swings, or ups and downs, known as *volatility*, can deliver a high return.

You can invest money in a company by purchasing an ownership stake, that is, buying stock or making a loan (buying a bond). Investments can also be made in commodities (gold, silver, oil, wheat, corn, and others) and real estate.

Individual stocks and bonds, mutual, or exchange traded funds (see below) are the vehicles or means of making these investments.

To begin making investments, you will need to open a brokerage account (see "How to Intelligently Use Financial Services").

You will likely have two investment accounts: a taxable and a non-taxable account. The taxable account will be a brokerage account maintained at a brokerage firm, while the non-taxable account refers to investments made inside a tax-deferred savings plan described in the previous chapter. The non-taxable account will likely be at a mutual fund company or at a brokerage firm, or possibly, though not likely, at a bank.

How to Invest in Your Taxable Account

Any funds invested in the stock market must be for a minimum of five years; otherwise, you run the strong risk of losing some of your money. You should use your bank account, not a brokerage account, to maintain your *operating* and *emergency* account or the accounts you will need to access day-to-day or week-to-week to cover your cash needs.

Investing principles:

1. The longer the time you have to make the investment, that is, the period for which you will not touch the money, the more aggressive you can be.
2. Aggressive refers to the percentage of equities or stocks vs. bonds in the account.
3. Bonds produce a fixed return with a high degree of certainty, while stocks produce a variable return with a low degree of certainty.
4. Stocks are more risky than bonds, meaning that over a defined period of time, you stand a greater chance of losing money with stocks than with bonds.
5. It is more risky to invest in an individual stock than in a mutual fund. A mutual fund represents an investment in thirty or more stocks; if one company does not do well, it will not have a great effect on your investment since you have many other investments within the mutual fund.
6. There are two components to your return on a stock: an increase in the price of the share (not certain) and a dividend paid (more certain) on the share. Most stocks, however, do not pay dividends; together these two pieces comprise the *total return* on a stock.
7. It is possible to lose money on bonds; it is important to be careful about the types of bonds you purchase.

8. The risk from the fixed return on a bond is that it will be less than the rate of inflation; the risk from the variable return on a stock is that you will sell the stock at a price lower than what you paid for it. Human nature would dictate against this, however, a psychological phenomenon causes many to interpret the most recent decline in the price as a harbinger of future declines, resulting in a sale at a price lower than the purchase price.

Depending upon how comfortable you are with variations (changes) in the value of your investments will determine how aggressive you should be. Generally, a time horizon of fifteen years or more, which all young people have, should result in a greater percentage of equities than fixed income in a *portfolio*, which is a group of investments. Below is an example of the *asset allocation* for a teen portfolio. The asset allocation refers to the division of investments in the portfolio. Past research has shown that it is the asset allocation that will have the most effect on determining what the investment return will be.

Portfolio Recommendation for a Young Person Aggressive Portfolio	
US Equities	
Large Capitalization Value stocks	18%
Large Capitalization Growth stocks	12%
Small Capitalization Value stocks	10%
Real Estate Investment Trusts (REITS)	5%
International Equities	
Large Capitalization EAFE stocks	20%
Small Capitalization EAFE stocks	15%
Emerging Market stocks	10%
US Government Intermediate Bonds	<u>10%</u>
	100%

EAFE = Europe, Australia, and Far East

Capitalization refers to the value of the company on the stock market. If you wanted to buy the entire company, that's how much it would cost. Market capitalization is calculated by multiplying the company's stock price by the number of shares that are traded on the exchange.

Large capitalization or "cap" for short are those companies which have a market capitalization of more than $10 billion, while *small cap* companies are those with a market capitalization of less than $10 billion.

Value stocks are companies which pay a higher than average dividend, while *Growth stocks* are companies paying a lower than average, or market, dividend, or which do not pay a dividend. The average dividend is based upon all the companies that are traded in the stock market. As previously noted, dividends are cash received from owning the stock; if you divide that cash by the price you paid for the stock, it gives you the *dividend yield*. For example, if the dividend yield for the entire stock market were 3.0 percent, then all those stocks with a dividend yield greater than 3.0 percent would be deemed Value stocks, while those with a dividend yield less than 3.0 percent would be considered Growth stocks.

Another way to distinguish between Value and Growth stocks is the ratio of the company's price in the stock market divided by its *earnings per share* (EPS is calculated by dividing the company's bottom line net income by the number of outstanding shares for that company). This ratio is referred to as the *price to earnings ratio* or P/E ratio. For example, if a company is trading at $15 and has an EPS of $1.00, then its P/E ratio will be 15x, that is the current price of $15 is "15 times" the current EPS. The P/E ratio represents the "multiple" investors are willing to pay to own one year of a company's earnings. The faster those earnings are increasing—think Apple—the higher the multiple. Once again, there is an average P/E ratio for the entire stock market, and those companies with a P/E ratio greater than the average are deemed Growth stocks, while those with a P/E ratio less than the average are deemed Value stocks.

It is important to distinguish between Value and Growth stocks because history has shown that, over time, Value stocks have produced a higher annual return than Growth stocks. That is due in part to the higher dividends paid by Value stocks; the dividends you get in cash are more certain and reliable than the possible increase in the price, which accounts for the majority of the return of Growth stocks. It is also due to the fact that Value stocks are cheaper than Growth stocks, providing the benefit of buying low.

Small stocks are those that have a market value or capitalization of less than $10 billion. A teen or young person should have a healthy representation of small stocks in their portfolio because over time, small stocks will outperform large stocks—this holds true both in the U.S. and overseas.

The reason small stocks outperform is because they are riskier than large stocks. In a capitalist economy, if you take on more risk, you have the potential to obtain a higher return.

Why is a small stock riskier than a large stock?

To answer this question, imagine if you had to drive cross-country in a small car, such as a Mini, and then imagine you have to make the same drive in a Hummer. When you make this trip, you are required to drive at least 10 percent of the time on dirt roads. Which car do you think will break down?

Small companies are somewhat like the Mini, they are strongly affected by changes in the economy in the same way the Mini will likely break down on a dirt road with many bumps and crevices. The Hummer, on the other hand, is not so much affected and is able to continue its journey until it gets back on a paved road. The Hummer is like a large company, not as affected as the small company by changes in the economy.

Therefore, small companies are riskier, in that they have fewer alternatives if something bad happens. Because they are riskier, they have the potential to provide you with higher returns over longer periods in the same way a Mini will drive better than a Hummer on a smooth road.

Why should you invest outside the U.S.?

Because most of the money in the world is outside of the U.S.!

That's not to say the U.S. isn't big; it is. It is just that all the other countries, when combined, are bigger than the U.S. In fact, if you added up the value of all the stock markets in the world, the U.S. stock market, as of

August 2010, would represent about 30 percent and the rest of the world about 70 percent of the total.

What are the other major stock markets around the world?

After the U.S., the next largest is in Japan, where the Tokyo Stock Exchange is located. The United Kingdom (England) with its market in London, called the London Stock Exchange, is the fourth largest. Germany, France, and Hong Kong also have large, well-developed stock markets.

There are some countries that are growing faster than others; they include China (third largest stock market), India (eighth largest), and Brazil (tenth largest), all of which have stock markets, which are newer and less well developed than the others. These countries are also called *emerging markets* because their economies are said to be emerging from the less developed into the developed world. The less developed world represents countries with lower levels of income per citizen, while the developed world, which covers the U.S., Europe, Japan, Australia, and Canada, has higher levels of income per citizen.

In addition to expanding investment opportunities outside the U.S., there is another reason to invest outside the U.S., and that has to do with something called *diversifying* your investments. This is the same as the saying "Don't put all your eggs in one basket," meaning don't invest in just one area because things may be not be going so well there. If you invest in Europe, Japan, China, India, and elsewhere, in addition to the U.S., then if the U.S. gets into trouble, for example, a recession, not all of your money will be subjected to the problem.

How to Implement a Young Person Investment Program

The best way to invest in the stock market is not to buy stocks.

The best, or least risky and lowest cost, way to invest in the stock market is through mutual and exchange traded funds, hereinafter referred to as "funds."

The easiest way to visualize what a fund does is to recall the old Greyhound Bus advertisement that said, "Leave the driving to us," which is what a fund does. Here the "driving" refers to implementing an investment program; when you do it through a fund, most of the work is done for you.

An investment program involves two tasks: (1) determining which investments to put in your portfolio (hard part) and (2) figuring out how to implement or execute the program (not as hard intellectually but requires more operational time).

As previously stated, investing in an individual stock or bond is more risky than investing in a fund that invests in stocks or bonds. For example, if you decide to have 15 percent of your portfolio invested in small stocks, you can buy a small capitalization fund that will purchase fifty or more small stocks.

Without getting too technical, the reason mutual and exchange traded funds are safer goes back to the "not putting all your eggs in one basket" concept.

A brief review of mutual and exchange traded funds

A mutual fund is a company organized to make investments, therefore, it is an *investment company*. Each mutual fund company is organized to make investments in specific parts of the stock market, that is, the fund's *investment objective*; for example:

Examples of Mutual Fund Investment Objectives:

- U.S. large capitalization stocks
- U.S. small capitalization stocks
- International large capitalization stocks
- U.S. government bonds
- U.S. corporate bonds

Therefore, each mutual fund company has an investment objective, which it must follow.

Each mutual fund company hires an investment advisor to manage the investments it will buy. For this service, the investment advisor is paid an *investment management fee*, which on average is 1 percent of the company's assets per year.

The mutual fund company sells its shares to the investing public, such that the money of many investors is "pooled" together in the mutual fund company. The investment advisor to the mutual fund company does all of the work in deciding which investments to purchase, within the objective of that particular fund. The shares of the mutual fund company are sold through brokers or directly by the company itself. Unlike a stock, which trades continuously throughout each trading day, the shares of the mutual fund company are bought and sold once at the end of each trading day after the market has closed.

An *exchange traded fund* operates in the same way as a mutual fund company except that its shares are traded continuously, that is, a price to buy or sell is available throughout the trading day (9:30 AM to 4:00 PM Eastern Standard Time) in the same way a stock is. Shares of an exchange traded fund company can only be purchased through a broker and, therefore, a commission will be charged.

When you purchase shares of a mutual fund company directly from the company itself, there are no trading commissions charged. For example, an account could be opened directly with Vanguard, one of the largest mutual fund companies in the U.S., and Vanguard will sell the shares directly to you without charging a trading commission. On the other hand, each time you purchase shares of stocks or exchange traded funds from a broker, you will likely have to pay a trading commission. These commissions vary depending upon the broker, but will range from $7 for an online broker such as E*Trade to upward of $30 or more for a traditional full service broker such as Merrill Lynch. Despite the potentially higher trading costs, exchange traded funds have other advantages as described below.

Another advantage of funds over individual stocks is that you save on trading commissions. Let's go back to our example where it was decided to invest 15 percent, or $15,000, of a portfolio in small cap stocks. On the one hand, you could purchase one index fund that invests in small cap stocks and pay one commission. Alternatively, if twenty individual small cap stocks were purchased, trading commissions would be charged twenty times. Let's compare the costs more closely.

Stock Trading Commissions:

	Commissions	Annual Fund Fees
Purchase small cap index fund	$18	$23
Purchase twenty individual stocks	$340	$ 0

Therefore, it would take more than eight years for the costs of purchasing and owning an index fund to equal the up-front commissions of purchasing stocks.

Of course, when you purchase the individual stocks, you have to be sure you are buying the right stocks. With the small cap index fund, you don't have to worry that the fund is buying the right stocks since it owns all of the small cap stocks!

As noted elsewhere, there are two types of mutual funds: *actively managed funds* and *index funds*. Actively managed funds try to beat the performance of the stock market as a whole by doing research to try to find the best companies, that is, those companies with stock prices that will potentially increase the most. Index mutual funds, rather than doing research to select only a few stocks, will purchase all of the stocks in a particular index in order to produce a return that exactly follows the index. Therefore, index mutual funds have lower investment management fees (they don't have to do research or travel to meet with the company) and other costs than actively managed funds. On average, the *expense ratio* for actively managed funds that purchase U.S. stocks is about 1.2 percent per year, while the expense ratio for index mutual funds purchasing the same type of stocks is about .25 percent per year; the investors or shareholders in those funds pay these expenses.[27] Expense ratios measure the cost to you of owning a fund, and are computed by dividing the fund's annual expenses by its assets. For example, if you invest $5,000 in a fund with an expense ratio of 1.2 percent, $60.00 will be deducted from your account each year. The return on a fund is computed after the $60.00 has been deducted—if the fund earned

6 percent during the year (the gross return), your return would be 4.8 percent which is the figure reported to you.

If the actively managed funds charge more, do they produce a higher return?

Historical data comparing the performance of actively managed funds to the stock market index shows that over periods of five, ten, or fifteen years, it is very difficult for an active manager to surpass the performance of the index. Morningstar, a company that provides information about stocks, funds and bonds to investors, produced data that shows only 40 percent of active fund managers were able to surpass the performance of the Vanguard Index 500.[28] Furthermore, the funds that beat an index during one year are not the same ones that do it in the succeeding year. Therefore, if you were selecting funds and chose the ones based upon their performance during 2008 in the hope they would do the same for 2009, you would likely be disappointed.

Exchange traded funds do the same thing as index mutual funds, that is, each fund is created to invest in a particular index.

What are the investment indices used by index funds?

Stock market indices are measures of the performance of one part of the stock market. The most important stock market indices are:

Standard and Poor's 500 Index (S&P 500): This measures the performance of the five hundred largest stocks in the U.S. traded on the New York Stock Exchange, American Stock Exchange, or the National Association of Security Dealers Automated Quotes, and are ranked according to their market capitalization.

Dow Jones Industrial Average: The Dow measures the performance of thirty large stocks in the U.S.; all of the companies included in the Dow are also in the S&P 500.

Wilshire 5000: The Wilshire 5000 measures the performance of the five thousand largest stocks, ranked according to their market capitalization, which are traded on the NYSE, AMEX, or the NASDAQ.

NASDAQ 100: The NASDAQ 100 measures the performance of the one hundred largest stocks, ranked according to their market capitalization, which are traded on the NASDAQ.

Russell 2000 Index: The Russell 2000 or "R2K" measures the performance of the two thousand smallest stocks in the U.S.; the stocks are ranked by their market capitalization.

Morgan Stanley Capital International Europe, Asia, Far East Index: The MSCI EAFE index measures the performance of the largest stocks, as ranked by their market capitalization, from the developed countries in Western Europe, UK, Japan, Australia, and Canada.

Morgan Stanley Capital International Europe, Asia, Far East Small Cap Index: The MSCI EAFE Small Cap Index measures the performance of small stocks, as ranked by their market capitalization, from the developed countries outside of the U.S.

Morgan Stanley Capital International Emerging Markets Index: The MSCI Emerging Markets Index measures the performance of large stocks, as ranked by their market capitalization, from the less developed or emerging market countries such as China, India, Brazil, Russia, and others.

When someone refers to the performance of the U.S. stock market, he is usually referring to either the S&P 500 or the Dow. The S&P 500 is more representative of the performance of the entire market since its five hundred companies account for over 75 percent of the total value of all stocks traded in the U.S. The Dow covers only thirty stocks and is much less representative of overall performance. When someone is referring to the performance of small stocks, they are usually referring to the Russell 2000.

Taxes

Exchange traded funds have another advantage over index mutual funds relating to taxes. The tax advantage of exchange traded funds, however, only pertains to ETF investments made in a taxable account or any account that is not an IRA or IRA rollover.

The tax problem with mutual funds originates when a shareholder or investor, other than you, wants their money back from the fund. When this happens, the mutual fund has to sell some investments in order to raise the cash to pay back the other investor. When this happens it is possible a capital gain is realized, assuming the price of the investment sold was greater than the initial purchase price. Because mutual funds distribute all of their income (a capital gain is investment income, see below) to the shareholders or investors, even though you did not sell, you will receive a distribution that you will have to report and pay capital gains taxes on. This does not happen with an exchange traded fund since, as we noted previously, its shares trade continuously throughout the day and, therefore, when someone wants their money the exchange traded fund doesn't have to sell an investment, the investor simply sells their shares through the market to someone else.

Selecting the Investment Products in a Young Person Investment Portfolio

Now that we have selected the type of investment products, what are the specific products to use?

Let's look at the products according to their *asset class*, which is a group of stocks or bonds that behave similar to one another and are, therefore, grouped together as one investment.

Asset Classes and Recommended Investment Products
U.S. large cap Value stocks
<ul><li>Vanguard Value ETF</li><li>iShares S&P 500 Value ETF</li><li>WisdomTree Large Cap Dividend ETF</li></ul>
U.S. large cap Growth stocks
<ul><li>Vanguard Growth ETF</li><li>iShares S&P 500 Growth ETF</li></ul>
U.S. small Value stocks
<ul><li>iShares Russell Small Value ETF</li><li>Vanguard Small Value ETF</li></ul>

US Real Estate Investment Trusts

- Vanguard REIT ETF

International large stocks

- iShares MSCI EAFE ETF
- iShares MSCI EAFE Value ETF
- WisdomTree International Large Cap Dividend ETF

Emerging market stocks

- iShares MSCI Emerging Market ETF
- WisdomTree Emerging Markets Value ETF

International small stocks

- WisdomTree Small Cap Dividend ETF
- Vanguard International Small ETF

ETF = exchange traded fund

When you open the account, you will want to ensure that all dividends received are re-invested into the respective funds and not added to the money market cash fund within the account; this is accomplished by checking the relevant box on the brokerage account application.

The specific amounts invested in each asset class will vary according to your specific risk profile.

Tax Implications for a Young Person Investment Account

How your investment account is taxed will be dependent on whether you file your own tax return or whether you are claimed as a dependent on your parent's return.

First, let's understand what is taxed in an investment account.

Investment accounts produce four types of income. Only two, dividends and long-term capital gains (capital gains result when you sell an investment for more than you paid; these gains are long-term if the investment was held for more than one year), currently receive preferential tax treatment or rates lower than ordinary income (salary) rates. The other two, interest income and short-term (investments sold in less than one year) capital gains, are taxed as ordinary income.

Investment Income:

- Dividend income
- Interest income
- Capital gains income – short term (less than one year)
- Capital gains income – long term (greater than one year)

Let's first look at the situation if you are claimed as a dependent on your parent's return. If this is the case, then you probably have a UTMA or a UGMA account.

While the UTMA/UGMA account lists one of your parents as the custodian, the investment income noted above will be taxed at your (lower) rate up until it reaches an annual inflation adjusted threshold—currently $1,900; after that, it will be taxed at your parent's (higher) rate. The meaning of taxed at your rate or your parent's rate pertains to those components of income, that is, *ordinary income*, which do not have lower, more favorable tax rates.

Preferential Tax Rates on Investment Income:

- Qualified dividends are taxed at a rate of 15 percent.*
- Long-term capital gains are taxed at a rate of 15 percent.*

* Reflects tax law as of July 2010. For 2010, those in the 10% and 15% rate brackets have a 0% qualified dividend and long-term capital gains tax rate.

Ordinary income refers to all other (not investment) income and is taxed according to the rate tables as per your income level. Therefore, if your only income is from the investment account and it is below the threshold, you will be taxed at your lower rate, whereas if the income from your investment account is above the threshold it will be taxed at your parent's, higher rate.

If you file a tax return on your own - you are not claimed as a dependent on your parent's tax return - you will be taxed on your investment income as follows:

1. Short-term capital gains, interest income and non-qualified dividends will be added to your salary (if any), together comprising ordinary income, and will be taxed according to your rate bracket.
2. Long-term capital gains and qualified dividends will be taxed at the current preferential rate of 0 or 15 percent.

Qualified dividends are those paid by companies that actually pay taxes to the U.S. government. Therefore, if that company also pays a dividend to its shareholders then the shareholder receiving that dividend will receive preferential tax treatment in the form of a rate of 15 percent rather than the ordinary income rate determined by their tax bracket.

Mutual fund investment companies are taxed differently than normal operating companies. A normal operating company, for example, Caterpillar, which, as you might know makes earth-digging equipment, may decide to pay some dividends from their net income with the remaining amount re-invested in the company. Investment companies, on the other hand, are required to distribute all of their earnings each year to their shareholders. Their earnings consist of dividends, interest, and capital gains from their investments, all of which are distributed or sent to the shareholders each year. Therefore, they pay no taxes to the government; all of their taxes are paid by their shareholders, on their individual tax returns, who receive the investment income.

If you file your own tax return then at the end of the year, the brokerage firm will send you a 1099 form, which shows interest, dividends, and capital gains realized in your account for that year. It is necessary you include this information on your tax return since a copy of this information is sent to the IRS. Their computers will check that the tax return with the Social Security number identified by the brokerage firm as receiving this income reports the same income on its return.

Different Forms of Business Entities
What Type of Company Should I Use in Starting a Business?

Understanding how business entities are legally organized provides insight into: (i) how they are taxed, (ii) how you are taxed as an owner and (iii) the degree of liability borne by the owners—all important considerations if you are going to invest in such entities.

In addition, those with the entrepreneurial bug must understand these issues prior to launching a new venture, particularly if third-party capital is to be accessed.

There are five basic types of business entities:

Types of Business Entities:

- Sole Proprietorship
- C Corporation
- Limited Partnership
- Limited Liability Company
- S Corporation

Sole Proprietorship

Most businesses in the U.S. are started as a sole proprietorship. In this method, there is no legal difference between the business and the founder.

What does it mean there is no legal difference between a founder and their company?

In business, legal entities or beings are "persons" who can enter into contracts, agreements, own things, and so on. In a business sense, "persons" are not simply human beings, but also non-human persons such as corporations and partnerships.

Therefore, when a sole proprietorship is established the owner and the business are one in the same. Many businesses are established using this method because it is fast and easy. You register the name of the business with the U.S. Patent and Trademark Office, secure an Internet domain, and open the business.

While the ease and short time to set things up are advantages, a sole proprietorship has a major drawback. Because there is no legal distinction between the founder and the business, there is also no separation for legal liability purposes. Consider the following example:

> Mike opens a bicycle shop where he sells high-end road or racing bikes. The shop is called "Mike's Bikes" and Mike is the sole owner. Mike invested $50,000 into the business to buy inventory and open the store, which is located across from the local university. Mike also owns a condominium nearby which he recently purchased for $275,000. To help transport the bikes, Mike owns a Ford F150, which he bought for $27,500. Bob purchased one of Mike's bikes and on a training ride, the frame broke, causing Bob to fall off and break his arm and leg and incur other injuries. Bob sues Mike for selling a defective frame and a jury awards Bob a $250,000 judgment. In satisfying the award, Mike will first use his business assets; the business provides $40,000 by liquidating the inventory. Now the problem arises; because Mike and his business are the same from a legal perspective, the balance of the award must come from Mike's personal assets. This requires Mike to sell his condominium in order to come up with the remaining $210,000 to pay Bob.

In summary, though a sole proprietorship is quick and easy, it exposes the business owner's personal assets to legal liabilities created by the business.

C Corporation

Creating a corporation protects the owner's personal assets from the legal liability of the business. This is accomplished because the corporation is a separate legal entity apart from the founder. It is called a "C corporation" because it elects to be taxed under Subchapter C of the Internal Revenue Code.

Because a corporation is a separate legal entity, certain steps have to be taken to create it, among them are:

- Articles of Incorporation
- By-laws
- Registration of corporation with the state

In organizing the corporation, the following items must be addressed:

1. *Board of Directors*: How many, responsibilities, meetings, minutes, compensation, etc.
2. *Par Value for Stock*: The initial value for the stock issued to the founders.
3. *Corporate officers*: Who will be president, secretary, treasurer, etc.
4. *Bank account*: As a separate entity, a bank account will have to be opened for the corporation.
5. *State of incorporation*: Founders must choose a state in which to incorporate and register the corporation.

You may have to hire a lawyer to draft the Articles of Incorporation, or you can use an online site that will do this for you, such as www.legalzoom.com.

Let's go back to our example of Mike's Bike Shop to see how a corporate form of ownership would have helped Mike.

Mike decides to incorporate, Mike's Bike Shop, Inc., in the State of Delaware. He chooses Delaware because its laws are more favorable to businesses in that it has statutes or rules that protect people who own businesses from their creditors. That means if the corporation later borrows money from a bank and has trouble repaying it, Delaware provides greater protection against the bank foreclosing or taking the business from the owner in order to repay the loan. Mike invests the same $50,000 into the business, but now receives common stock, issued by Mike's Bikes, Inc., evidencing his ownership of the business. When Bob sues this time, the jury awards the judgment against Mike's Bike's Inc., not Mike personally. Since Mike's Bike, Inc., only has assets worth $50,000, this is all that is paid. In other words, the judgment cannot go through Mike's Bikes, Inc., to Mike personally; instead, it stops with the corporation and Mike's personal assets, house, and car, are protected and safe. The corporate form of ownership has protected Mike's personal assets.

Are there any drawbacks, other than the time and cost, to a corporate form of ownership?

Yes.

The problem with a corporation is when a dividend is paid to the stockholders; the issue is that the dividend is taxed twice. Because a corporation is a separate entity, it has its own tax liability and must file its own tax return separate from the return the owners file. A corporation pays dividends with "after-tax" money, that is, with funds, which have already been taxed. When the shareowners receive the dividends, they must include them in their gross income and pay tax on it. Therefore, the dividends are taxed twice—*double taxation of dividends*—the first tax is paid by the corporation, which distributes the dividend, and the second tax is paid by the individual who receives the dividend.

Let's see an example:

Mike's Bikes, Inc., had a good year, and paid $25,000 of dividends to Mike, the sole owner. Mike Bikes, Inc., paid taxes at a rate of 39 percent on the money it earned, from which it paid the dividend. Mike paid taxes at a rate of 15 percent on the dividends he received from the business. Therefore, for each dollar Mike's Bikes, Inc., sells and ultimately pays as a dividend $0.39 goes to pay corporate taxes while $0.15 of tax is paid by Mike on his personal return for each dollar of dividends he receives—not a good way to get money from a corporation to its owners!

Most of the businesses you will invest in through the stock market are organized as C corporations.

Partnership

Owning a business through a partnership structure enables you to avoid the double taxation of dividends problem faced by a corporation and the legal liability issue created by a sole proprietorship.

Partnerships are fairly easy to establish, though they do require a partnership agreement. This agreement details the relationship between the two parties in a partnership: the general and the limited partner.

The *general partner* is responsible for the day-to-day management of the partnership, while the *limited partners* have no role in managing the day-to-day affairs of the business, but are the people who put up the money for the business to operate. They have what is referred to as a passive role in the partnership, kind of like a "silent" partner.

"Flow-through" accounting

Like a corporation, the partnership itself is a distinct legal entity such that any liability of the business is confined to the assets of the partnership—it does not extend to the personal assets of the partners. Unlike a corporation, the partnership has no tax liability of its own; rather, all of the profits or losses are "flowed through" to the partners according to their respective ownership percentages. This is known as *flow through accounting* and is the main advantage of the partnership form of ownership.

The partnership agreement will also detail the profit split between the general and the limited partners. Typically, the general partner will receive 20 percent of the profits, while the limited partners will receive 80 percent of the profits. The share received by the general partner is their compensation for the day-to-day management of the business. The partners will receive their profits via cash distributions or non-cash allocations to their capital account from the partnership. These distributions will be reported to the IRS by the partnership through the issuance of a K-1 form. This form, sent to all partners, shows the amount of profits each partner must report on their individual tax return, and also shows their adjusted ownership in the partnership. It is absolutely necessary for each partner to report this on a return because the IRS is receiving the same information. Computers will match the payment to the recipient's Social Security number to see if it has been reported on their return.

Cost of a partnership interest: The "basis"

When a partner invests in a partnership, the cost of the investment becomes his or her "basis," which is how partners are able to measure profits and to calculate taxes when the investment is sold. Each time a partner receives a profit distribution, this increases the basis; when a loss distribution is received, it reduces their partnership basis. These changes to the original basis are known as the *adjusted basis*. When the partner sells a partnership interest, the amount of tax calculated is based upon the difference between the sales price and the adjusted partnership basis.

Master limited partnership interests are traded on the New York Stock Exchange and can be bought and sold, similar to a corporate stock. Most of these limited partnerships own and operate energy storage and distribution businesses.

Limited Liability Company

Limited liability companies (LLCs) are the newest form of business owner-ship. They are similar to partnerships in that they incorporate flow through accounting and liability protection for the company's investors or owners. The advantage of a limited liability company is greater flexibility for the roles of the investors. For example, the investors in a limited liability com-pany are known as "members" who can also serve in the day-to- day opera-tions of the business and, thus, be a "manager." Therefore, the LLC form of ownership allows a "member-manager" to both invest in and manage the business.

As stated, the LLC form of ownership is the newest type of business and was only recently adopted by all of the fifty states as an acceptable form of business ownership.

S Corporation

Owning a business via an S corporation structure provides the same benefits as an LLC or partnership, however, there are more restrictions regarding the shareholders in the business. An S corporation is identical to a C corporation except that it elects to be taxed under Subchapter S of the Internal Revenue Code—the income of the corporation is not taxed but rather the income or loss is passed pro-rata to the shareholders, thus, avoiding the double taxation of dividend problem cited above. Some of the restrictions are that the company must be a domestic company, there can be no more than seventy-five shareholders, and no foreign nationals can be shareholders. Other than the shareholder restrictions, the S corporation functions in similar ways to the partnership or LLC structure.

Chapter Fourteen

What should a teenager know about economics?

Would knowledge of basic economics help teens make better decisions and benefit the overall economy?

What beneficial lessons about economics would a teen carry forward into adulthood?

Would that benefit the economy?

How Economics Affects Personal Finances

Most fundamentally, economics is about using the price mechanism to increase or reduce the supply of a good. Make something more expensive and you will get less of it; make it cheaper and you will get more of it.

In the U.S. and most other industrialized countries, the economy consists of three sectors that interact with one another: consumers, government, and business.

In a market economy, businesses produce, consume, and sell goods and services; consumers buy goods and services; and the government buys, regulates, and taxes goods and services. If you add together the total value produced by consumers, businesses, and government, you get something called the *Gross Domestic Product* or "GDP." Changes in the GDP are used as a measure to determine whether the economy is growing or contracting. In the U.S., the largest component of the GDP is consumer buying, which accounts for about two-thirds or 66 percent of the total.

Easier lending standards and real estate speculation

Consider the concept of how prices result in supply and demand adjustments and think about mortgages. Prices of mortgages are the rate of the loan, which is subsidized by the tax deduction for mortgage interest. Therefore, easier lending standards, in effect, reduced the price of a mortgage, resulting in an increase in supply or availability of mortgages. An increase in the availability of mortgages, on the other hand, directly affected the price of houses in that it put more buying power into the system. Such increased buying power resulted in the real estate bubble of 2003 to 2006, which artificially bid up housing prices.

If people had connected the increased availability of mortgage financing to the run-up in housing prices, perhaps fewer would have bought into the speculative bubble, resulting in lower delinquencies and foreclosures.

Stock trading and personal wealth

Another area is the stock market, specifically trading costs. If you lower trading costs, you get more trading; more trading results in higher commissions, lower returns, and less wealth. Since fixed commissions were abandoned in May 1975, discount brokerage firms, pioneered by Charles Schwab & Co., Inc., have driven down trading costs. This resulted in increased trading with no appreciable increase in returns. Studies have shown that the returns earned by individual investors trail the market returns with more frequent trading exacerbating the deficiency. In a study done in Finland, it was shown that more frequent traders earned returns 53 percent less than investors who traded less.[29]

An understanding that lowering the cost of something brings more of it might have lead people to understand that increased stock trading and the whole "day trading" episode were a consequence of lower trading costs, not a greater ability to make stock market trading profits.

Subsidizing college costs

Certainly, many studies show the benefit of a college education on lifetime earnings. There are many other occupations with pay commensurate with that of an individual with a bachelors degree, yet such professions are not deemed "high end" and are shunned by many young people. Such professions include electrician, carpenter, plumber, auto technician, and lawn care professional.

A plethora of programs are available to help finance a college education—Pell Grants (government grants which do not have to be repaid), Stafford loans (subsidized and un-subsidized government loans), Hope credit (tax credit), tax-advantaged 529 accounts, and Coverdell Education Savings Accounts (tax-deferred educational savings accounts). These programs contribute to increasing students' buying power and ultimately the number of college freshmen competing for the fixed number of spaces in a freshman class. Not only does this push up the price for those attending college, but it also makes it easier for colleges to justify tuition increases.

If college financing was less accessible, then perhaps some would pursue these other professions or perhaps college tuition increases would be moderated. This, in turn, might result in higher wage growth both in professions requiring a college education, for example, middle level corporate managers, administrators, and other professionals, and in those not requiring a college education, such as those listed above. This might happen because the supply of professional managers would be reduced, driving up their price. While the supply of vocational workers would be increased, this might result in higher quality work, because of a greater pool of skilled professionals in these fields, tending to moderate the downward pressure on wages. People are willing to pay higher prices for jobs well done, notably in fields where there is tangible evidence of superior work, for example, a beautiful garden or lawn, professional carpentry, and so on.

State regulation of health insurance

One of the reasons health insurance premiums are high is due to the lack of supply in local markets. Lack of supply owes to restrictions on purchasing health insurance across state lines. This prohibition prevents consumers from reaping the benefits of competition, as only a few companies are able to offer health insurance in each state. There are close to one thousand health insurers in the U.S., yet in any one state, usually only five to ten health insurers offer policies.

Money and Credit

Young people also need to understand the basics of our financial and banking system in order to better assess the impact of governmental policies on them. Since teens and young people are big users of credit, in relation to their net worth, understanding the impact of governmental policies regarding interest rates would help to improve their finances.

This can easily be done by watching the actions of the Federal Reserve Board or the Fed. The Fed's primary focus is to maintain stable prices; that is, to make sure inflation, or a general rise in prices, does not move beyond their target range.

The Fed measures the rate of inflation via monthly changes in the *Consumer Price Index* or "CPI." They exclude two items from the gross CPI they feel causes the index to be too volatile: food and energy costs. Once they remove these two items, they come up with a CPI – Core Index (the gross index less food and energy.) The Fed then has a target range for changes in the CPI Core; currently this range is 2 to 3 percent annual increases. When the CPI Core monthly increases are close to the 3 percent upper bound on an annualized basis, it is likely the Fed will be increasing interest rates in the months ahead because it is concerned about inflation. On the other hand, if the annualized monthly increases in the CPI Core are close to 1 percent or even if they show a decrease, the Fed is less likely to take action (because it is more concerned about rising prices than with falling prices or deflation). Deflation, however, associated with a recession will cause the Fed to lower short-term interest rates.

How do changes in short-term interest rates affect young people?

Changes in short-term interest rates affect credit card rates, auto loan rates, and some mortgage rates. Those mortgage rates affected will be adjustable rate mortgages, which are tied to a short-term interest rate such as Treasury bills or the *London Interbank Offered Rate* or "LIBOR."

LIBOR is an "inter-bank" interest rate, in that it is the rate banks with excess funds charge to other banks that borrow these funds. LIBOR rates range from overnight, the loan is made one day and repaid the next day, up to one year later. While LIBOR refers to London, it is a reference point for short-term interest rates around the world.

How does the Fed change short-term rates?

The Fed has three ways it can effect a change in short-term rates:

> ### How the Fed Changes Rates:
>
> - Changes to the discount rate
> - Changes in reserve requirements
> - Open market operations

These three methods are referred to as the tools of monetary policy. *Monetary policy* along with fiscal policy, which is concerned with changes in government spending and tax rates, are the primary tools the government uses to try and move the economy one way or another. Monetary policy uses changes in the *money supply* to affect the economy. The money supply is the amount of money in the economy available for people to spend. People get money to spend either by earning it through a salary or via loans from banks. When you use a credit card, the bank has made a loan to you; banks also lend money directly to individuals to buy homes and indirectly by making loans to companies. Companies in turn use these loans to buy things and pay salaries to their employees.

By far, the most important tool of monetary policy is *open market operations*, which works in the following way.

Bank assets consist of loans to individuals and companies as well as U.S. government securities. U.S. government securities include Treasury bills, notes, and bonds. When one buys a Treasury bill, they are making a loan to the U.S. government for a period of up to one year, while a Treasury note is a loan to the U.S. government for up to ten years. These loans are made by banks buying securities issued or sold by the U.S. government. A security is simply a loan that can be traded on an exchange. The U.S. Treasury Department is the part of the government that sells these securities.

Through open market operations, the Fed will either buy or sell these government securities held by the commercial banks. When the CPI-Core is close to the upward bound of the acceptable range, the Fed will act to increase short-term interest rates by reducing the money supply. It will conduct its open market operations by selling government securities to commercial banks. When commercial banks purchase these securities, they transfer cash from themselves to the Fed, in effect, reducing the money supply and increasing interest rates. Conversely, when the Fed wants to reduce interest rates it purchases government securities from commercial banks transferring cash from itself to the banks, increasing the money supply and reducing interest rates.

What is fiscal policy and how does it affect young people?

Fiscal policy is the other tool the government uses to affect the economy. With both fiscal and monetary policy, the government's objective is full employment with stable prices. Full employment means an unemployment rate no greater than 3 to 4 percent; stable prices means, as noted above, increases in the annual consumer price index of no more than 3 percent.

Whereas monetary policy is conducted by a small group of people, the Board of Governors of the Fed, fiscal policy is conducted by Congress and the President. Fiscal policy refers to changes in tax rates and government spending to achieve the full employment/stable price objective.

The U.S. tax code is a lengthy set of regulations regarding tax rates, allowable deductions, and credits. The most important changes Congress and the president make to tax laws and government spending or fiscal policy are:

1. Ordinary income tax rates or the amount of taxes you have to pay on your salary
2. Type and amount of deductions allowed in calculating adjusted gross and taxable income, above and below the line deductions
3. Corporate tax rates
4. Amount of money the government will spend to build highways, bridges, schools, courthouses, airports, and other "infrastructure" investments
5. Benefits the government pays to people who are out of work, including the time and amount of money an individual can collect unemployment payments
6. Amount of time an individual can continue to obtain health insurance from their previous employer

Unlike monetary policy, changes to fiscal policy require a lengthy amount of time as Congress and the president have to agree on the policy. Changes to monetary policy occur much quicker as the Federal Reserve Board of Governors meet frequently and can make changes at any of their meetings.

As a young person entering the job market, or a newly hired person, you need to be aware of how fiscal policy can affect you.

Any changes to ordinary income (salary) tax rates will impact any raise you get. Getting a salary raise that puts you in a higher tax bracket, may result in you seeing less cash in your paycheck than you expected. If feasible, it might be worthwhile to speak with your employer about getting a non-monetary increase such as increased life insurance paid by the employer, better retirement benefits, or lower out of pocket payments for health insurance.

Changes made to tax deductions may affect your expenses. For example, if changes are made to the mortgage interest tax deduction, it will make your out-of-pocket costs of a mortgage loan more or less expensive. Depending on where you live, it may also affect rental rates in that these changes may force people in or out of the rental market.

When the government spends money to build a highway, it gets the money in one of two ways: borrowing it by selling treasury securities or raising taxes to pay for it. Either way, you get affected. When the government borrows money, it increases the demand for money; as you know, increasing the demand for something will drive up its price and in this case, the price of money goes up which means higher interest rates.

Increasing unemployment benefits, in effect, subsidizes, or makes cheaper, leisure or non-work. States administer unemployment programs such that an increase in unemployment benefits in a particular state may make it easier to find a job in that state because more people find it easier and less expensive to stay out of the labor force, thus, reducing competition for jobs.

International Economics

What are some of the items you may purchase that are made outside the U.S.?

Teen Purchases of Products Manufactured Outside
of U.S.:

- *Car* – Japan, Mexico, Germany, South Korea
- *Jeans* – El Salvador, Sri Lanka
- *iPhone/iPad* – China, India (software)
- *Beer* – Mexico, Netherlands
- *Eyeglasses* – China, Italy
- *Watch* – Hong Kong (China)
- *Sneakers* – Malaysia, Sri Lanka, Mexico

How does it affect me if the things I buy are made outside the U.S.?

Let's examine a Samsung HDTV made in South Korea. Samsung pays the workers who assemble the HDTV as well as the components that go into the HDTV in the currency of South Korea, which is called the won. When Best Buy imports, purchases, a product from outside the U.S. for sale into the U.S.—the HDTV—they have to pay Samsung in won because Samsung needs the won to pay their workers. Therefore, Best Buy must get won to pay Samsung. They do this by selling dollars and buying won in the *foreign exchange market.* Using the current exchange rate for won into dollars, Best Buy calculates how much they should charge you in dollars.

Each day, the amount of won obtainable for $1.00 changes, based upon the supply and demand for won and dollars in the foreign exchange market. If the price of won goes up such that we get less won per $1.00, then we say the won has appreciated vs. the dollar.

For example, if last week we were able to receive 1,225 won per $1.00 and this week we were only able to get 1,110 won per $1.00, then the won has become more expensive. If the won gets more expensive, Best Buy has to sell more dollars to get the amount of won needed to purchase the HDTV.

For example, if the price of the HDTV is 1,163,750 won, then at an exchange rate of 1,225 won per $1.00, Best Buy has to sell $950 to pay for the HDTV. However, if the exchange rate depreciates to 1,110 won per $1.00, then Best Buy has to sell $1,048 dollars to pay for the HDTV, representing a price increase of 10 percent!

Therefore, the price of the dollar relative to that of other currencies will affect the price of things you buy. If the dollar depreciates then the dollar prices for goods manufactured outside of the U.S. will increase to you.

What makes the price of the dollar depreciate?

As stated, the price of U.S. dollars vs. other currencies is determined in the foreign exchange market, which operates much like other markets according to the laws of supply and demand. What then makes people want to buy more or less dollars?

People around the world desire to purchase dollars because the U.S. is the largest and most powerful economy in the world. For that reason alone, people from overseas desire to purchase dollars. In addition, people around the world are seeking to invest in places that pay the highest interest rate. Therefore, if interest rates in the U.S. are higher than those in, say, Australia, people will buy U.S. dollars, which will also cause the price of U.S. dollars to increase compared to the Australian dollar.

Finally, when Best Buy had to sell dollars to buy won, this too caused downward pressure on the dollar vs. the won. The aggregate amount of trade between two countries is recorded as the *trade balance*. If more U.S. companies are selling dollars to buy won in order to import South Korean products, then the U.S. will have a trade account deficit with South Korea and this will put downward pressure on the dollar, or cause the dollar to depreciate vs. the won. The opposite would happen if companies in the U.S. were selling more—exporting to—South Korea than they were purchasing. In that case, South Korean companies would be buying dollars (selling won) in order to get the dollars to buy Boeing jets for South Korean airlines, for example.

When investors outside of the U.S. purchase dollars in order to buy U.S. Treasury bonds, they also affect interest rates in the U.S. Their actions will not affect the rate you pay on your credit card as much as it might affect the rate on your mortgage. As stated above, when the U.S. government borrows money by selling Treasury bonds in order to build a highway, this puts upward pressure on long-term interest rates because it increases the supply of bonds. With the same demand for the bonds, the government has to increase the interest rate on its bonds to get people to buy them. Mortgage rates are based on interest rates on Treasury bonds, specifically the ten-year Treasury bond. Because the U.S. government is the safest entity to lend money to, the rate on the Treasury bond will be the base rate, and mortgage rates will be set at a level above Treasury bonds since it is riskier to lend money to you to buy a house than to the government to build a highway. If investors outside the U.S. are now buying Treasury bonds, because the rates are higher than government bonds in their own country, then demand for Treasury bonds has increased and the Treasury doesn't have to raise its interest rate as much in order to sell the bonds.

What makes the U.S. dollar different from other currencies?

Fundamentally, the dollar is the world's reserve currency. This means that the default choice for foreigners with excess funds is to invest those funds in dollar denominated assets—primarily U.S. government Treasury bills and bonds, and to a lesser extent U.S. stocks and real estate.

Being the world's reserve currency also means that many transactions occurring in the world outside of the U.S. are denominated in dollars. For example, when Saudi Arabia sells oil to Australia, the Australians pay for the oil in U.S. dollars. This means Australians will first have to buy the U.S. dollars, which will push up the price of U.S. dollars vs. the Australian dollar in the foreign exchange market. When a business executive wants to rent an expensive apartment in Mexico City, most likely the price will be quoted in U.S. dollars, which requires the executive to first exchange his or her pesos for dollars, again causing the price of the dollar to rise vs. the peso in the foreign exchange market.

Chapter Fifteen

SOLUTIONS TO THE PROBLEM: RECOMMENDATIONS FOR
FINANCIAL LITERACY INSTRUCTION IN THE U.S.

At What Age Should We Begin Teaching Our Kids about Finance?

Children become aware of the economy at roughly ages nine to ten, when they begin to understand the role of money as a medium of exchange. They begin to understand that one has to do something productive to get money.

To understand some of the basics of finance, an understanding of algebra is needed. In addition, a cognitive understanding of abstract ideas is also required.

Therefore, the ideal starting point for teaching personal finance is the beginning of high school in ninth or tenth grade.

Who Should Teach Finance to Teens?

Finance can be a very dry subject; I know because I teach it to college students.

To keep it fresh requires weaving real world situations into black and white concepts in order to stimulate interest and heighten attention and focus. When I speak to my class, it is easy to see students perk up when I refer to something in the paper that day, just as easy as it is to see them doze off when I monologue about theory and concepts from a book.

Therefore, it is essential that instructors teaching finance to teens have real world experience. A teacher who relies solely on explaining book concepts without being able to illustrate these with their own experiences will find it hard to maintain attention, focus, and interest among students.

Where Would Teachers with Financial Experience Be Found?

Financial professionals such as Certified Financial Planners must maintain their certification by providing continuing education credits every two years. As part of this requirement, the CFP Board could require high school finance instruction at the practitioner's local high school as part of the continuing education requirement. Not only would this supply a source of highly qualified professionals, but it would also connect practitioners to their community.

Public schools would have to budget this as an additional teacher, which would require sign-off from the local school board and teachers union. Given such hurdles, it is likely that financial instruction would first be introduced into charter schools where principals have a freer hand in selecting teachers and curriculum.

An alternative to using existing financial professionals would be to select teachers who would complete the educational requirements for a Certified Financial Planner. Local financial planning firms could form partnerships with local school boards to employ teachers in order to give them their real world experience requirement before going back and teaching finance in the high school.

Such a partnership between local school boards and financial planning firms would also benefit other teachers, as those teachers who become professionally trained would be able to offer professional financial advice to teachers who need it. I have several teacher clients and know firsthand of the lack of professional financial advice now available to teachers.

What Curriculum Should Be Offered?

Recommended curriculum for a high school personal financial literacy program is:

1. *Moving Money through Time*: Understanding the time value of money as a basis to calculating needed savings to purchase items in the future; effect of different rates on required savings

2. *Markets and the Role of Issuers and Investors*: Understanding how money flows from those who have it to those who need it

3. *U. S. Financial System*: Major players in U.S. economy—who they are and how they interact with one another; how it affects one's financial well being

4. *Using Financial Services*: Basics about the use of checking and investment accounts, insurance, understanding how financial products are sold, how to purchase financial products, using professional financial advisors vs. doing it yourself

5. *Budgeting*: Creating and using a personal financial budget

6. *Investing*: Different investment vehicles; creating and managing a portfolio

7. *Taxes*: What taxes will I have to pay, what are taxes used for, how to complete the 1040 form

8. *Credit*: Understanding credit cards, annual percentage rates, effective annual rates, mortgage loans, loan amortizations

9. *Global Financial System*: How events overseas affect one's financial well being in the U.S.

10. *Young People and Retirement*: Understanding the importance of tax-deferred savings plans as a key way to build wealth; create awareness so young people, when entering their first job, will take advantage of programs to reap full benefits rather than ignoring them as only something for old people

Learning Format

I firmly believe that you learn by doing.

Financial literacy needs to be taught by engaging students in real world exercises that drive home the topic being taught.

Within the above curriculum, real world exercises such as the following need to be offered:

Moving Money through Time: Calculate how much you need to save each month in order to buy a car in three years, assuming a 4 percent rate.

Markets, Issuers and Investors: Groups of students assume and play-act roles necessary for a corporation to sell stock through the NASDAQ; roles would be financial team at a company, regulators at NASDAQ and SEC, investment bankers, and pension fund purchasers.

U.S. Financial System: Students assume the role of the Federal Reserve Open Market Committee; they are presented with economic data and must formulate a monetary policy response.

Alternatively, students prepare a budget for the U.S., which addresses different economic scenarios, for example, inflation, recession, stagflation, declining U.S. dollar, rising interest rates, and so on.

Using Financial Services: Students complete forms to open bank and brokerage accounts; financial product advertising is reviewed for accuracy and truthfulness; students go online to shop for auto insurance; students evaluate the costs and benefits of using different financial professionals.

Budgeting: A personal budget is prepared, problems in staying on budget are discussed, and solutions are offered to get back on track.

Endnotes

1 U.S. Department of Labor, *Consumer Expenditures*, April 2009, U.S. Bureau of Labor Statistics.

2 "Project on Student Debt," May 4, 2007, www.projectstudentdebt.org/pub_ view.php.

3 David Godsted and Martha Henn McCormick, "National Adults Financial Literacy Overview," Networks Financial Institute at Indiana State University, August 2007, p. 3.

4 Applied Research and Consulting, LLC, "NASD Investor Literacy Survey."

5 Charles Schwab & Co., Inc., "Teens & Money Survey," 2007.

6 Jump$tart Coalition for Personal Financial Literacy, February 2008.

7 Craig Copeland, "Individual Account Retirement Plans: An Analysis of the 2007 Survey of Consumer Finances, with Market Adjustments to June 2009," Employee Benefit Research Institute, August 2009.

8 Dalbar, Inc., "Quantitative Analysis of Investor Behavior Study of 2005."

9 Anamaria Lusardi and Olivia Mitchell, "Financial Literacy and Retirement Preparedness: Evidence and Implications for Financial Education Programs," Michigan Retirement Research Center, University of Michigan, December 2006.

10 Dana Markow and Kelly Bagnaschi, "What American Teens and Adults Know about Economics," The National Council on Economic Education, April 26, 2005.

11 U.S. General Accounting Office, "Consumer Finance: College Students and Credit Cards." Publication No. GAO-01-773, June 2001.

12 S. Joo, J.E. Grable, and D.C. Bagwell, "College Students and Credit Cards." In J.M. Hogarth, ed., *Proceedings of the Association for Financial Counseling and Planning Education*, 2001: 8-15.

13 Michael E. Staten and John Barron, "College Student Credit Card Usage," Credit Research Center, Georgetown University, working paper #65, June 2002.

14 D.L. Tan, "Oklahoma College Student Credit Card Study," Norman, OK: University of Oklahoma, Center for Student Affairs Research, 2003.

15 The Hartford, "New National Survey Finds Parents Concerned about Children's Financial Independence," April 14, 2008, press release.

16 "NASD Investor Literacy Research," Applied Research and Consulting, April 2003.

17 "What Americans Know about Economics," National Council on Economic Education by Harris Interactive, January-February 2005.

18 Joyce Jones, "College Students Knowledge and Use of Credit," American Association for Financial Counseling and Planning Education, 2005.

19 Ibid.

20 "Credit Card Consumers: College Students Knowledge and Attitude," *Journal of Consumer Marketing* 17 (2004): 617-626.

21 Investment Company Institute, www.ici.org/pdf_flows_2009.pdf.

22 "NASD Investor Literacy Research," Applied Research and Consulting, 2003.

23 John C. Bogle, "Mutual Fund Industry Practices and their Effect on the Individual Investor," statements made before the subcommittee on capital markets, U.S. House of Representatives, March 12, 2003.

24 Jane J. Kim, "Low Fees Outshine Fund Star System," The Wall Street Journal, August 8, 2010.

25 "ICI 401(k) Participant Activity," Investment Company Institute, March 9, 2009.

26 Annuity 2000 Mortality Tables

27 "Index Funds vs. Actively Managed Funds," bankrate.com, November 15, 2007.

28 "Index Funds vs. Actively Managed Funds."

29 Ben-Cohn Urbach and Joachim Westerholm, "Trading frequency, investor returns and behavioral biases," University of Sydney, 2007.

Author Biography

 ERIC J. WEISS, CFP®, AIF® serves as Chief Investment Officer and president of Brightscape Investment Centers, Inc. Prior to founding the company he directed the business development activities of Chase Manhattan Bank's Global Asset Management and Private Bank Division in northern Latin America. Previously, Mr. Weiss was a senior executive at Citicorp's corporate finance group in New York and Latin America. Mr. Weiss earned his M.B.A. from the University of Chicago where he interned at the Center for Research in Security Prices (Chicago, IL) under the direction of Professor Myron Scholes, a Nobel Prize recipient for his work in option pricing. Prior to his studies at Chicago, Mr. Weiss earned an M.A. in economics from Columbia University where he wrote his thesis under the direction of Robert Mundell, also a Nobel Prize recipient for his work in international monetary economics.

Mr. Weiss holds the Series 65 investment advisor license, is a member of The National Association of Personal Financial Advisors (NAPFA) and has been named one of "America's Top Financial Planners" by the Consumer's Research Council of America.

Index

1040 form, 74-75
1099 form, 101
12b-1 fee (mutual funds), 65
401(k) plan, 11-12, 66-67, 84
403(b) plan, 83-84
457 plan, 83-84
529 account, 113

A

ABA number, 57, 58
Above-the-line tax deduction, 74
ACH transfers, 58
Actively managed mutual funds, 64, 95-96
Adjustable rate mortgage, 7, 14, 19, 114
Adjusted Gross Income (AGI), 74
After-tax cost of an expense, 75
Annual percentage rate (APR), 34
Ask price, 61
Asset allocation, 89
Asset class, 98
Auction Rate Securities, 44
Auto insurance, 48

B

Balloon payment (loan), 23, 32
Below-the-line tax deduction, 74

Bid price, 61
Bond, 13-14, 18
Bounced check, 52
Bridge financing, 41
Broker, 54
Brokerage account, 54
Broker-dealer, 54
Budget, 25

C

C corporation, 105
Capital, 28
Capital gains tax, 64
Capital purchase, 28
Capitalism, 43
Capitalization (stocks), 90
Certified Financial Planner, 122
Charles Schwab & Co., Inc. 112
Check 21 system, 59
Check cashing services, 68
Closed-end mutual fund, 62
Collateral, 8, 9, 35
Commissions (stocks), 55
Compounding, 12, 23, 85
Confused Debt Cycle, 68
Consumer Price Index (CPI), 114
Coverdell Education Savings Accounts, 113
Credit (uses of), 40
Credit card, 16, 31, 52

Credit score, 31
Custodial brokerage account, 57

D

Defined benefit pension plan, 11, 12, 66, 86
Defined contribution pension plan, 65
Delinquency rate (credit card), 16
Disability insurance, 50
Discount broker, 55
Diversifying investments, 92
Dividend yield, 90
Dividends, 90, 100
Double taxation of dividends, 106
Dow Jones Industrial Average (DJIA), 96

E

Earnings per share (EPS), 90
Effective annual rate (EAR), 23, 34, 51
Emergency account, 88
Emerging markets, 92
Employee Benefit Research Institute, 11, 81
Employer match - 401(k), 84
Equity mutual fund, 13
Exchange rate, 40
Exchange traded fund (ETF), 92-94, 98
Expense ratio (mutual fund), 63, 95

F

Federal Deposit Insurance Corporation (FDIC), 54
Federal Reserve (Fed), 37, 114

Federal Reserve Clearing System, 58
Federal Reserve System, 52
Federal Reserve Wire Network, 58
Fee-only compensation (financial advisors), 57
FICA, 73
Fidelity Investments (mutual fund company), 83
Fiduciary standard, 56
Fiscal policy, 116
Fixed income, 14
Flow-through accounting, 107
Foreign exchange market, 118
Free cash, 28
Full service broker, 55
Future value (FV), 15, 28, 29

G

Government securities, 115
Gross domestic product (GDP), 111
Growth stocks, 90

H

Health insurance, 49-50
Health savings account, 49, 75
Hindsight bias, 43
Hope credit, 113

I

Income tax, 71
Index mutual funds, 64, 95-96
Individual brokerage account, 57
Individual retirement account (IRA), 11-12, 74-75, 81

Inflation, 19, 39
Interest (on a loan), 32
Interest income, 100
Interest only loan, 23, 32
Interest rate, 9, 18, 23
Intermediaries (financial), 37
Investment company, 93, 101
Investment Company Institute, 44
Investment management fee (mutual fund), 94
Investment objective (mutual fund), 93
Itemized (tax) deduction, 75

J

Joint brokerage account, 57

K

K-1 form, 107
Keogh plan, 11, 83

L

Large cap stocks, 90
Life insurance, 24, 47
Limited liability company (LLC), 108
Liquidity, 5, 11, 13
Loan amortization, 32, 53
London Interbank Offered Rate (LIBOR), 114
Long-term capital gains, 100
Long-term capital gains (taxes), 101
Long-term care insurance, 50

M

Making a market, 61
Market economy, 35
Medicaid, 73
Medicare, 73
Minimum required payment (credit card), 53
Monetary policy, 38, 115
Money supply, 115
Morgan Stanley Capital International EAFE index, 97
Morningstar (investment information company), 96
Mortgage interest tax deduction, 117
Multiple (stock market), 90
Mutual fund, 19, 20, 93-94, 98

N

NASDAQ, 60
NYSE, 60
National Association of Securities Dealers (NASD/FINRA), 18, 54
Negative amortization (loan), 14, 23
Non-refundable tax credit, 76

O

Open market operations, 115
Open-end mutual fund, 62
Ordinary income (taxes on), 100, 116-117
Overdraft line, 52

P

Partnership, 107
Partnership basis, 108
Payment function (PMT), 28
Payroll tax, 72
Pell Grant, 113
Pension, 12
Pension Benefit Guaranty Corporation (PBGC), 86
Periodic compounding (interest), 33
Personal auto policy (PAP), 48
Personal Operating Profit (POP), 26
Personal Operating Profit margin, 27
Plan sponsor (pension plan), 84
Portfolio, 89
Present value (PV), 28
Price to earnings ratio (P/E), 90
Principal (loan), 32
Prospectus, 63

Q

Qualified dividends, 101

R

Refundable tax credit, 76
Registered investment advisor, 56
Registered representative (rep), 56
Revenue sharing (mutual funds), 55, 64
Risk profile, 99
Rollover IRA, 84
Roth IRA, 83
Russell 2000 Index, 97

S

S corporation, 109
S&P 500 Index, 13
Securities and Exchange Commission (SEC), 63
Securities Investor Protection Corporation (SIPC), 54
Self Employment Pension (SEP), 83-84
Series 65 (securities license), 56
Series 7 (securities license), 56
Short-term capital gains, 100
Short-term capital gains (taxes), 101
Single limit coverage auto insurance, 48-49
Small cap stocks, 90
Social Security, 12, 20, 72
Sole proprietorship, 103
Split limit coverage auto insurance, 48
Stafford loan, 113
Standard and Poor's 500 index, 96
Stock exchange (NYSE) specialist, 61
Stocks, 13
Suitability rule, 56

T

Tax credit, 76
Tax liability, 74
Taxable income, 74
Tax-deferred account, 81
Tax-deferred investing, 83
Taxes, 22
Tax-filing status, 78
Term life insurance, 47
Ticker symbol (stocks), 60
Time value of money, 27

Total return (stock), 88
Trade balance, 119
Trade settlement (stocks), 62
Turnover-stock trading, 64

U

U.S. Treasury bonds, 119
Uniform Gifts to Minor Act account (UGMA), 44, 57, 100
Uniform Transfers to Minor Act account (UTMA), 44, 57, 100

V

Value stocks, 90
Vanguard (mutual fund company), 83, 94

W

Withholding (paycheck), 73